Just Enou

Just Enough

Just Enough
Sufficiency as a Demand of Justice

Liam Shields

EDINBURGH
University Press

Edinburgh University Press is one of the leading university presses in the UK. We publish academic books and journals in our selected subject areas across the humanities and social sciences, combining cutting-edge scholarship with high editorial and production values to produce academic works of lasting importance. For more information visit our website: www.edinburghuniversitypress.com

Edinburgh University Press Ltd
The Tun – Holyrood Road
12(2f) Jackson's Entry
Edinburgh EH8 8PJ

First published in hardback by Edinburgh University Press 2016

Typeset in 11/13 Sabon by
Servis Filmsetting Ltd, Stockport, Cheshire
and printed and bound by CPI Group (UK) Ltd
Croydon, CR0 4YY

A CIP record for this book is available from the British Library

ISBN 978 0 7486 9186 9 (hardback)
ISBN 978 1 4744 3260 3 (paperback)
ISBN 978 0 7486 9187 6 (webready PDF)
ISBN 978 0 7486 9188 3 (epub)

Contents

Acknowledgements and Dedication

An acknowledgement in a monograph is a rare opportunity for an academic to be self-indulgent and sentimental. In the main, good academic work is characterised by the single-minded, dispassionate pursuit of truth and knowledge. In that pursuit one must keep one's feelings to oneself and kill one's darlings. But self-indulgence is not all bad and often sentimentality is uniquely appropriate when giving thanks and acknowledging one's debt.

In writing this book I have incurred debts of varying sizes to a large number of people. These debts go back a long way.

I would like to begin by thanking my parents Ged and Dawn Shields, who have supported me in every possible way. The thought that this achievement would make them proud was a constant source of strength.

I have been fortunate to have been a member of groups of political theorists and political philosophers at several institutions. I would like to thank the Philosophy and Politics departments at Keele University and the Politics department at the University of York for making the study of political philosophy seem irresistible to me. Thanks is owed to Glen Newey, Paul Bou-Habib, Monica Mookherjee, Mat Matravers, Tim Stanton, Jon Parkin and David Edwards. I would especially like to thank John Horton at Keele who encouraged me to study the subject further and nurtured my interest in sufficientarianism when supervising my undergraduate dissertation.

My main academic debt is to Andrew Williams, who supervised my PhD thesis, on which some of the chapters are based. His penetrating criticisms, detailed comments and helpful suggestions have made me the political theorist I am today and have greatly improved the argument within the book. I owe a significant debt to Fabienne Peter, who became my supervisor at a time when I was struggling to clarify my thoughts. Under her close supervision I quickly overcame my difficulties. Without her input, in particular on the chapter on autonomy, this book would certainly have been much worse.

I would also like to thank two anonymous reviewers at *Utilitas* for two rounds of detailed comments on a paper based on the arguments of Chapter 1. These comments have greatly improved my understanding of sufficientarianism and the arguments contained in this book.

A large number of people at the University of Warwick have helped me whilst writing the thesis. For their help and encouragement I would like to thank Enrique Camacho, Stephen Butterfill, Kai Spiekermann, Stephen Houlgate, Eileen John, Alex Sutton, Keith Wilson and Chris Godfree-Morrell. Special thanks should go to those with whom I have had extensive discussions about all or part of the thesis. These include Matthew Clayton, Ed Page, Chris Clarke, Douglas Bamford, Victor Tadros and all members of the Centre for Ethics Law and Public Affairs, University of Warwick. I have benefitted enormously from several conversations in various public houses and curry houses with Tim Fowler, Adam Slavny, Dean Machin and Brian McElwee. Furthermore, the examiners of my PhD, Adam Swift and Zofia Stemplowska, gave me invaluable comments both in my viva voce examination and in the aftermath.

In the academic year 2013/14 I took up a one-year postdoctoral research position at the McCoy Family Center for Ethics in Society at Stanford University. Not only did this provide a glorious physical environment in which to research, but the Center's weekly workshop was an excellent forum for discussion of work in progress. I am extremely grateful to Lily Lamboy, Chris Lewis, Ben Miller, Sara Mrsny, Erin Cooper, Debra Satz, Eamonn Callan, Rob Reich, Brent Sockness, Anne Newman, Kristi Olsen, Jorah Dannenberg, Allison McQueen, Tamar Schapiro, Brian Berkey, Will Braynen, Mark Budolfson, Hyunseop Kim, Julie Rose, Patrick Taylor-Smith and Alex Levitov for helping me with aspects of this book through conversation and written comments.

I am especially grateful to Alex Levitov and Patrick Taylor-Smith for their help with the chapter on global justice.

Since January 2012, I have been a member of staff in the Manchester Centre for Political Theory (MANCEPT). I think this must be one of the best places anywhere in the world to be a political theorist and I am grateful to all of my co-members for their help with my research. I would especially like to thank Miriam Ronzoni, Christian Schemmel, Stephanie Collins, Stephen Hood, Nici Mulkeen, Joe Horton, Steve de Wijze, Richard Child, Hillel Steiner, James Pattison, Chris Mills, Dean Redfearn, Jon Quong and Tom Porter-Sinclair.

I have also collected a number of debts outside any institutional affiliation I have held. I am grateful to David Axelsen, Lasse Nielsen, Robert Huseby, Luara Ferracioli, Iwao Hirose, Sarah Hannan, Thomas Rafferty, Emily McTernan and Martin O'Neill for discussions of sufficientarianism and related matters. I am especially grateful to Paula Casal, not only for writing the paper 'Why sufficiency is not enough', which has influenced me greatly, but also for helping me along the way anonymously, as well as Philipp Kanschik and Rudolf Schüßler for inviting me to the University of Bayreuth to present at a conference on sufficientarianism where I learned a great deal from audiences and presenters.

Finally, I dedicate this book to my wife Claire Shields. Marrying her was the best thing I ever did.

1 Politics and Distributive Justice

Ours is a world of shortage and excess. Some people do not have enough food and water to live on. Others do not pay enough tax. At the same time some people have much more than enough food and wealth, and some people even pay too much tax. A failure to secure enough of some goods is relevant to the moral appraisal of our world, including our actions and the design of our social, legal and economic institutions. It is often the case that we *should* ensure that people have enough of some goods.

The idea of sufficiency is the subject of this book, which provides a clarification and defence of sufficiency as a demand of social justice and draws out its implications for some practical debates, such as those concerning educational provision, child-rearing and our obligations to the global poor. Prior to any deeper analysis of sufficiency, and its possible role(s) in practical debates, I must say something about the background to the debates that I am addressing and how sufficiency and other ideas about social justice fit into them.

Politics and Distributive Justice

Political philosophers are interested in questions of justice. They are interested in what justice demands of individuals and social institutions. These questions are essentially a matter of evaluating political subject matter, which on the broadest understanding includes individual actions in the private sphere and also the design of institutions. It is understood that the appropriate standard for assessment is one of justice. To adapt the words of John

1

Rawls, beliefs should be *true* and societies should be *just*. If beliefs are not true, then we should change them. If societies are not just, then we should change them too. To know what kinds of change should occur and to evaluate whether societies, including existing ones, are as they should be, we require an account of what justice demands. Only then can we see if our society measures up to it.

Evaluating the actions of politicians and governments is a popular pastime outside of the academy. People regularly pass judgement on who we *should* vote for, what the laws *should* be and how the tax burden *should* be shared. Such evaluations are popular partly because we realise that they are important. How the tax burden is shared really matters to us. It really matters how access to important medical treatment and university education should be determined, and not only because of our own self-interest. That is, not only because we might need medical treatment or because we might want free university education for ourselves. We do not answer these questions selfishly. These questions matter because it is important that we are treated in a defensible and just manner regardless of how it affects our narrow self-interest. In making these judgements about these policies we make implicit judgements about the demands of justice that ground them.

The way political philosophers grapple with these questions is characterised by greater rigour and devotion than many non-professional philosophers have the time to achieve, but the questions are the same questions that inspire debate and discussion in public houses across the land. Thus, the relevance of political philosophy goes beyond the academy, beyond parliament and city hall, and into the streets as well.

One way that political philosophers have thought about answering questions about the demands of justice is in terms of sharing between members of a society the goods and resources that are available. This way of understanding justice is called 'distributive justice' and it is the focus of this book.[1] Distributive justice concerns the way that goods and resources like education, wealth and opportunities for well-being are distributed or made available to us. Whether a society is just, or not, and how it can be more just is a function of how these resources are distributed. If these resources are distributed in accordance with sound principles, then society is just, and if not, then justice demands that we rearrange the distribution in a way that better satisfies those principles. Principles of distributive justice, then, can help us to work out whether society is just or not, but they can also help us to decide what we should do to improve things, by changing the laws and policies that can affect this distribution. Thus, the principles of distributive justice have a role in both *assessing* alternatives and *guiding* future decisions. These principles underlie the everyday judgements we make about stories in the news.

Those working on distributive justice have drawn mainly on the notion of equality, providing arguments that goods or resources should be distributed equally. The influence of equality as the distributive ideal can be seen in each of distributive justice's two central questions. The first is Amartya Sen's question, 'Equality of what?'[2] This question asks, 'If equality is the correct way of distributing benefits and burdens, then what should be distributed equally?' This is a question about what has been called the 'currency of justice', which is concerned with how we should understand the significance of the various benefits and burdens we can share.[3] Part of the reason why it is so important that we work out what stuff we should, fundamentally, be concerned with the distribution of, is that distributing one thing equally means that some other thing is distributed unequally. If I were to give two people equal shares of money, they would be unequally happy with the result since people typically have different, and more or less expensive, tastes than each other. Thus, we must choose what it is that we want to equalise. The 'Equality of what?' question is not my main concern but I shall survey some answers briefly because any complete distributive principle will have some currency.

Broadly speaking, there have been three different answers to the 'Equality of what?' question. One answer that has been given is welfare or opportunity for welfare.[4] Welfare is supposed to capture what it means for your life to go better. Welfare can be cashed out in terms of utility or pleasure, or preference satisfaction or through some objective list of goods.[5] Those egalitarians who claim that welfare is the currency of justice claim that we should favour policies that minimise inequalities in how well people's lives go, even if this means exacerbating income or wealth inequalities. The second type of currency is resources. Resources can include wealth and income, or particular goods such as land and cars, or they can be understood as including wealth, income, rights and liberties, and the social bases of self-respect. This last view is John Rawls's and he calls such resources 'primary social goods'.[6] Egalitarians who claim that resources should be the currency of justice are not concerned fundamentally with how well people's lives go, so long as they have equal resources. Thus, they support policies that promote equal shares of resources rather than equal shares of welfare. The third and final putative currency of justice is capabilities. Martha Nussbaum and Amartya Sen have claimed that the proper focus of distributive justice is not the outcome level of welfare achieved or the resources with which we can pursue our ambitions, but rather what functionings we are capable of achieving if we so wish.[7] Capability theorists deny that policies that help to equalise resources or welfare are to be pursued at the expense of policies which help to promote capability. There are various debates about the relative merits of these currencies of justice and there are debates about whether these currencies are even distinct from one another.[8]

One further option when deciding upon the currency of justice is to be a pluralist and employ several different currencies.[9] If we do so, we may claim that wealth should be distributed in accordance with one principle and welfare distributed in accordance with another. If we take such a route, we will have to explain what to do when these principles yield conflicting guidance. But this additional argumentative burden is not a decisive objection to pluralist theories.

This book focusses only indirectly on that first question and endorses particular currencies at particular times. The book focusses directly on the relative merits of answers to the other central question of distributive justice: 'Equality or what?', defending the answer: 'Sufficiency.'[10] Many political philosophers believe that equality is the correct way of distributing the currency of justice, whatever that is. Equality can be understood either as a satiable or an insatiable demand. Some have held a view that might be called 'simple equality'. Simple equality states that the currency of justice should be distributed equally and that the more equally it is distributed the better that society is in respect of justice. The simple equality view generates a satiable demand of justice. Satiable demands can be completely met in principle and once met, cannot be and could not have been met further. Simple equality provides us with a satiable demand because, while a distribution can be more or less equal, no distribution can be more equal than a perfectly equal distribution. If two people have ten euros each, then they have equal shares of euros. Their shares of euros could have been greater or lesser but, so long as they have ten each, they could not possibly be more equal. There is no more equality present when they each have ten, twenty or thirty euros.[11]

Insatiable versions of equality state that, as well as having reasons to prefer equality to inequality, we have reasons to prefer equality at a higher level to equality at a lower level because, at the higher level, there is more of the thing that is advantageous.[12] In contrast to satiable demands, insatiable demands can always, in principle, be met to a higher degree. Thus, consider a demand to maximise your earnings. It is always possible, in principle, to have greater earnings. There can always be more money in the world that could be yours, for example if we were more productive or if we printed more. Thus, a demand to maximise your earnings is insatiable and so a demand to achieve equality at the maximum level is also insatiable. On the insatiable equality view we should always strive for improvements.

Simple equality is indifferent between distributions in which everyone is equally well off and those in which everyone is equally badly off, while insatiable equality demands equality at the higher level. Thus, the two equality views can provide us with different practical guidance and are vulnerable to different objections.

It is worth noting a further family of egalitarian views that I do not take to be distributive, since they do not necessarily favour the equal distribution of anything. These views are egalitarian because they state that the just society is a society of equals or that citizens should be treated as equals.[13] This thought is compatible with vast inequalities along many of the dimensions we seem to care about. For instance, a view advocating equal and absolute property rights is compatible with such inequalities. Of course, we may criticise this view for not capturing our intuitions about equal treatment or equal concern, but we need further premises to do so. These views I call 'social egalitarian', though they are sometimes known as relational or democratic egalitarian, and I do not consider these views to be an answer to the question of how the currency of justice should be distributed since we can accept their claim that 'we should live in a society of equals' compatible with a wide range of familiar distributive principles. The social egalitarian merely provides a theme for our theorising and, on its own, cannot answer the difficult questions about how we should distribute the tax burden, how healthcare budgets should be spent and whether private schools are consistent with justice. This is not to say that there are no plausible social egalitarian theories of justice; it is simply to say that such a theory will rely on the independent plausibility of distributive principles, whether they are egalitarian or not, and so it is worthwhile to focus on the merits of those distributive principles directly.

An alternative to equality as a distributive ideal is the idea of priority.[14] The idea of giving priority to the worse off is a familiar one. Some political philosophers have claimed that justice demands that we give priority to the worse off when considering how the currency of justice is distributed even when this is less efficient and exacerbates inequalities. Principles of priority may offer different guidance from principles of equality in cases where incentives to some generate inequality but maximise productivity in ways that redound to the benefit of the least advantaged, in absolute terms. To explain, consider the following example. Imagine that if we promise to pay some people much more than others to do their jobs, they will work much harder. Their hard work translates into greater productivity in the economy and increases the resources and benefits in society that can be distributed. This allows us to improve the plight of the least advantaged in our society in ways that we simply could not without the productivity improvements generated by unequalising incentives. If we care about prioritising the worse off, rather than equality, then we should permit inequalities in income, such as those resulting from these incentives. Thus, equality and priority may give us different guidance and, since we should care about getting the correct guidance, we must find reasons to choose between them.

Versions of prioritarianism make the following claim: for any persons or groups X and Y, it is more important to benefit X than Y if X is worse off than Y in respect of the currency of justice. There are many versions of prioritarianism. *Weighted prioritarianism* claims that the weight of our reasons to benefit any person vary in proportion to how well off that person is. According to such a view, if I have two units of the currency of justice and you have four units, it is twice as important to benefit me by one extra unit as it is to benefit you by the same amount. In addition to attaching greater weight the worse off a potential recipient is, prioritarians can also attach weight to the size of benefits and the number of potential beneficiaries. Versions that do so will still insist that it is always more important to benefit the worse-off group rather than the better-off group when the potential benefits are equal and when the groups are equal in size. However, if there are more people in the better-off group, this may outweigh the priority given to the worse off, and if we can benefit the better-off group by a much greater amount, then this too may outweigh the priority given to the worse off. Thus, if we can benefit a small group of medical patients who have a terrible disease or a very large group of patients who have a mildly inconvenient ailment, it is an open question as to which group we should benefit. Proponents of weighted prioritarianism believe that the numbers matter in such cases and do not think that justice always requires benefitting the worse off, no matter what.

Proponents of *absolute prioritarianism* claim that factors like the size of the group or the size of the benefit are not relevant to how we ought to distribute benefits and burdens.[15] These views claim that we should always give a benefit to the worse off even if it means large numbers of the better off lose out on very large benefits. On this view, we should benefit a tiny number of people who suffer with a terrible disease rather than a very large group with a mildly inconvenient ailment. And we should do so for the reason that they are worse off. I will be discussing some of these views in detail in later chapters.

There are many other ways benefits or burdens might be

distributed, other than in accordance with principles of equality and priority. Principles of desert claim that we should distribute the currency of justice to each according to what he or she deserves.[16] On this view, the more deserving should be better off than the less deserving. Principles of aggregation claim that we should change social arrangements so as to yield the greatest aggregate sum of that currency.[17] Utilitarianism is an example of such a principle, and versions of it insist that we should arrange things so as to maximise the amount of utility or pleasure in society, regardless of its distribution between different people. However, I will not focus on these views. I will focus on sufficientarian principles of distributive justice and their merits relative to what I take to be their strongest rivals, that is, principles of equality and priority just introduced.

Sufficientarianism is so called because members of this family of principles appeal to the idea of sufficiency in making evaluations of distributive justice. Sufficientarians claim that securing enough matters when we evaluate the way goods are distributed within society. The idea that it is important to secure enough is a familiar demand from ordinary conversations. In our daily lives, we often appeal to the importance of getting enough sleep, or having enough time to perform a particular task. However, sufficientarian principles are less frequently discussed and advocated than principles of equality and priority have been. This book seeks to clarify the most plausible accounts of sufficientarianism and defends the claim that in matters of distributive justice we should take sufficientarian principles as our guide.

At this point a question may arise in readers' minds: 'Why do we need principles? Why not just make it up as we go along? We already have a good idea of what is just and what is unjust.' My answer is that while we think we do have a good idea of what is unjust and perhaps some of the things that justice requires, such as fairness, we do not have much reason to be confident in ad hoc judgements and even if we did, those judgements often conflict. Moreover, it is precisely where we need guidance most that our intuitions are unclear. One reason for appealing to a principle for guidance is that we require consistent guidance. We cannot get consistency by appealing to our intuitions, or at least we cannot be confident that we will get consistency. Two inconsistent guiding judgements cannot possibly be correct. Thus, we are justified in applying the more plausible consistent set of judgements. The most plausible principles are those that can explain our convictions where we are most confident, for example regarding slavery as an injustice, and can give us guidance with the most difficult cases, for example regarding the permissibility of inequalities that are to the benefit of the most disadvantaged. That a principle works in the obvious cases gives us reason to be confident in its ability to get the right answer where our intuition is unclear or silent. We certainly should not follow principles that get it intuitively wrong in the obvious cases. Thus, in order to address the real practical problems we face, we need principles that we can have confidence in to offer us guidance in the tricky cases.

My defence of sufficiency as a demand of distributive justice employs the method of *reflective equilibrium*.[18] This method requires an appeal to principles and intuitions in order to find a satisfying balance. Sometimes I must revise the principle because it clashes with particular convictions; at other times I must revise my intuitions or convictions about a case when no plausible principle can be found to support it. Overall, we try to get the most intuitively satisfying whole, using theories or principles to explain our intuitions about particular cases and particular cases to vindicate intuitive theories or principles. Throughout this book I take it that deeply implausible implications of a principle, such as recommending slavery, can be grounds for rejecting that principle as a good guide. More specifically, I aim to show that our convictions about particular cases, and our intuitions, are better organised and explained by an account of justice that includes sufficientarian principles than one that does not.

The approach of this book is comparative. I do not seek to show that some view can avoid some criticism, or that some criticism does apply to some view, as some academic work does. I am not really concerned with the absolute merit or absolute plausibility of sufficientarian principles. What really interests me is the question of which principles are more plausible than all the others. I am examining whether sufficientarian principles are more plausible than their rivals. This is because it is only when sufficientarian principles are more plausible than their rivals that they can be indispensable to a complete and sound theory of justice. Only then should we take sufficientarian principles as our guide in practical matters, such as public policy.

This interest sways my use of reflective equilibrium. The intuitions, convictions and cases I construct to elicit judgements of the plausibility of the views I consider are taken from cases where sufficientarian principles are distinct from their rivals. Only where such views provide distinct judgements or have distinct features can we tell them apart in terms of plausibility.

Prospectus

I have just elaborated the topic I will be discussing and the position I will be defending. I have also discussed my methodology. I will now provide an overview of what I will argue in the chapters that follow.

This book defends the claim that sufficiency has an indispensable and extensive role in a sound account of the demands of social justice. It does this by showing both that there are some sufficientarian principles that are indispensable in that they are more plausible than their rivals and that they should play an extensive role in our thought about practical debates. I have already explained the importance of indispensable principles, but the importance of having an extensive role in our thought may seem unclear or unnecessary. The prospects for sufficientarianism do not only depend upon there being an indispensable sufficientarian principle(s). They also depend on the extent of the role those principles should play in our thought about practical debates. The extent of the role a principle plays in our thought depends upon a number of factors including whether and how it fits with other plausible demands of justice and whether it can help to resolve some problems in relevant debates.

If a sufficientarian principle had little of significance to say in terms of policy implications, could not shed light on the various problems in those debates and did not fit alongside, or was always outweighed by, accepted and plausible demands in that area, then the principle could not have an extensive role in our thought. Such a principle would do less to improve the prospects for sufficientarianism than a principle that had important implications for policy, resolved some problems in various debates and could fit in well alongside some of the plausible demands of justice in the relevant areas.

In Chapter 2, I begin by defining what makes a distributive principle an interesting and important one. I claim that this depends upon whether such principles are indispensable to an account of justice and the extent of the role they play in our thought about practical debates. I clarify this by saying that indispensable principles are more plausible than their rivals where distinct from them. In the case of sufficientarian principles, the rivals are principles of equality and priority.

I then survey the way that sufficientarian principles have been understood and defended as demands of justice. I explain that the two main ways of understanding the special importance of securing enough are vulnerable to powerful objections, to which rival views are not vulnerable, and on this basis are thought less plausible than their rivals. I then examine whether sufficientarians can avoid these objections. I claim that a clearer understanding of sufficientarian principles, one more closely grounded in the way the ideal is invoked in ordinary usage, shows that sufficientarian principles can avoid these objections and so may have an important role in distributive justice and the relevant practical debates.

Sufficientarian principles are distinctive because they claim that it is important that people secure enough of some goods and that once enough is secured, there is a shift in our reasons to benefit people further. Neither of these claims renders them vulnerable to the main objections that have been made of sufficientarianism and so sufficientarianism may yet have an indispensable role to play in an account of justice.

Towards the end of Chapter 2, I claim that sufficientarian principles can be defended by two lines of argument. The first line of argument involves searching for the kinds of reasons that can support a shift. I call such reasons 'sufficientarian reasons' and if we have such reasons, then they will support some particular indispensable sufficientarian principle. The second line of argument involves searching for clashes of value, whereby giving absolute priority to either seems implausible and giving priority to sufficiency in one of those values offers a more plausible solution. The remaining chapters then defend specific sufficientarian reasons or specific value clashes, which support sufficientarian principles and draw out their implications for practical debates. Only if there are some indispensable sufficientarian principles that have important implications for practical debates can I succeed in showing the importance of sufficientarianism for justice.

In Chapter 3, I argue that a principle of sufficient autonomy is more plausible than the best rival principles, including non-sufficientarian and instrumental principles of autonomy, and as such is indispensable. I argue that we have a sufficientarian reason to live under the conditions of freedom, a satiable part of which is each individual possessing sufficient individual autonomy. This means that, as a demand of justice, each person has an especially weighty claim to secure sufficient autonomy and this should be respected in the design of laws, policies and the workings of the basic institutions. Thus, this principle can offer us sound guidance and assessment of our society and the government's actions that may threaten or promote sufficient autonomy.

In Chapter 4, I show that the principle of sufficient autonomy has interesting and important policy implications in the area of education. To do so, I consider the cases of curriculum design and school choice. I argue that the principle provides us with very important guidance and that in debates about the rationale for compulsory schooling and distribution of opportunities to develop talents, this principle helps to resolve difficulties that other principles alone cannot.

In Chapter 5, I argue that parents who provide their children with a good enough upbringing cannot usually be denied custody of them. I argue that parents have an interest in not being denied the right to rear and that the child has an interest in having the best upbringing. These interests clash where the child's current parents cannot or do not perform as well, with respect to the child's interests, as other willing candidates. I conclude that the most plausible resolution is to appeal to an account of the good enough upbringing constituted by those of the child's interests that are weightier than the adult's interest in retaining the right to rear. Thus, in addition to defending a claim for a good enough upbringing as an especially important requirement of justice, I specify this content of the good enough upbringing in a way that can inform policy. I show that the account of the good enough upbringing has very important implications for debates about child protection, and the practices of adoption and fostering. I do this by considering the criteria that are used by social services to remove children from the custody of their parents.

In Chapter 6, I turn to the possible role that considerations of sufficiency should play in global distributive justice. In this chapter I first set out the distinctive views that the shift-based approach to sufficientarianism makes available. I next show that some of these versions are more plausible than prevailing sufficientarian approaches to global justice. I then go on to demonstrate that some of the more radical sufficientarian approaches to global justice that are made available by the shift-based understanding of sufficientarianism have crucial advantages over non-sufficientarian approaches to global justice.

In the Conclusion, I summarise my main claims and make some suggestions about the future for sufficientarianism.

Notes

1. Lamont and Favor, 'Distributive justice'.
2. Sen, 'Equality of what?'
3. Cohen, 'On the currency of egalitarian justice'.
4. Arneson, 'Welfare should be the currency of justice'; Dworkin, *Sovereign Virtue*, 11–16.
5. Crisp, 'Well-being'.
6. Dworkin, *Sovereign Virtue*, 65–119; Rawls, *A Theory of Justice*, 54–5.
7. Nussbaum, *Women and Human Development*; Sen, 'Capability and well-being'.
8. Dworkin, *Sovereign Virtue*, 285–306.
9. Walzer, *Spheres of Justice*.
10. Here I echo Derek Parfit's Lindley Lecture 'Equality or priority?'
11. Raz, *The Morality of Freedom*, 235–44.

12. In Christiano, 'A foundation for egalitarianism', 73, the author states: 'I want to argue that since the truth of the proposition that more substantial good is better than less substantial good is a necessary condition for the truth of the principle of equality in the substantial good, the right account of the principle of equality must somehow include the idea that equalities in which everyone is better off are better than equalities in which everyone is worse off.'

13. For examples, see Anderson, 'What is the point of equality?'; Dworkin, *Sovereign Virtue*; Scheffler, 'What is egalitarianism?'; Schemmel, 'Distributive and relational equality'; Wolff, 'Equality: the recent history of an idea'.

14. Hirose, 'Reconsidering the value of equality'; Holtug, 'Prioritarianism'; Parfit, 'Equality or priority?'; Peterson and Ove Hansson 'Equality and priority', 301; Weirlich, 'Utility tempered with equality', 431–3.

15. In Rawls, *A Theory of Justice*, 72, the author states: 'in a basic structure with n relevant representatives, first maximise the welfare of the worst off representative man; second, for equal welfare of the worst-off representative, maximise the welfare of the second worst-off representative man, and so on until the last case which is, for equal welfare of all preceding n-1 representatives, maximise the welfare of the best-off representative man. We may think of this as the lexical difference principle.'

16. Sher, *Desert*.

17. Singer, *Practical Ethics*, 3.

18. Rawls, 'Outline of a decision procedure for ethics'; Scanlon, 'Rawls on justification'.

2 What is Sufficientarianism?

Political decisions typically involve making trade-offs.[1] Since there are limited resources available, there are finite means with which to achieve our aims. Sometimes politicians will have to decide whether to build more hospitals or more schools, enhance the military or increase benefits for pensioners. Often the choices will not be so positive. They may involve reducing the number of nurses or teachers or else cutting benefits to pensioners or forgoing military upgrades. As such, there are always winners and losers as a result of these decisions. Even where the trade-off is not zero sum, where we cannot make some better off without making some worse off, there are opportunity costs, and we have to be able to justify our decisions to those who miss out, even if they are no worse off. To make these trade-offs in the correct way requires giving due weight to the morally relevant factors, which may include individuals' rights, equality and sufficiency. When combined with accurate empirical data about the likely effects of implementing certain policies, these factors will guide us when considering what to do. While the empirical data will tell us whether a certain policy will enhance equality or sufficiency suitably defined, normative arguments tell us whether we ought to enhance equality or sufficiency. When making such decisions, then, we need some normative principles as our guide, and we need arguments to support them and give us confidence in one set of guiding principles rather than another. The ultimate aim of this book is to establish that sufficientarian principles will be part of the best set of guiding principles.

Before I can offer arguments in favour of sufficiency being part of this guide, we need an account of what a commitment to sufficiency as a demand of justice is. This chapter provides a clarification of sufficiency as a demand of justice, in the abstract, and shows how the objections that have been made to several attempts to defend sufficientarian principles can be avoided. To this end, I will provide a historical survey of sufficientarianism, presenting the two main ways that sufficiency has been understood as a demand of distributive justice. I show that each way of understanding sufficiency as a demand of justice is vulnerable to very powerful objections that have been made in the philosophical literature.[2] I will argue that such objections can be avoided. In order to show that these objections can be avoided, I provide a clear statement of the minimum claims that one must make if one believes that securing enough of some good, whatever that is, is a morally relevant feature of situations. I then show that the criticisms of past sufficientarian principles do not apply to all possible commitments to sufficiency as a distinctive and important demand of justice. This means that we can appeal to the special importance of securing enough and avoid these important objections. It then becomes an open question as to whether sufficiency should be our guide since sufficiency is not doomed from the start. I then set out the necessary and sufficient conditions of sufficiency being an important part of the principles that should guide us. In particular, I show that sufficiency should be our guide if we have certain kinds of (non-instrumental, non-egalitarian, weighty and satiable) reasons to secure more of some goods, since only sufficiency will be able to account for this. In later chapters, I will defend particular sufficientarian principles and show how they help us to deal with difficult trade-offs in the areas of global inequality, education and child-rearing. But first we must determine what makes a principle of justice sound, in general, regardless of whether it is sufficientarian in nature.

What Are Sound Principles of Justice?

What distinguishes the principles we should use as our guide in matters of policy from those we should not? Whether we should accept some principle of justice as our guide depends on whether that principle is *indispensable to* a sound and complete account of justice. When is a principle of justice indispensable to a sound and complete account of justice? A principle of distributive justice is indispensable only when we cannot do without it in the most plausible account of justice. The primary source of plausibility or implausibility is whether the implications of a principle cohere with our considered convictions of justice, which, though revisable in principle, usually confer credence on a principle. As such, to be indispensable, any principle of distributive justice, sufficientarian or otherwise, must offer more plausible guidance than the most plausible alternative principles or sets of principles. I call candidate alternative principles 'rival principles'. For sufficientarians, principles of equality and principles of priority are their rivals. Clearly, if any principles are less plausible than their rivals, we would not want, never mind need, to refer to them in a sound account of justice. Thus, indispensability hinges on whether certain principles are more plausible than their rivals. We can say more than this, however. For a principle to be more plausible than its rivals, it must be distinct from them in terms of the guidance that determines plausibility. If two principles offer the same guidance in all conceivable cases, then neither is indispensable. Indispensable principles will be distinctive and more plausible than their rivals where distinctive, since it is only where they are distinctive that the views can be told apart in terms of their plausibility.

The main rivals I have in mind throughout this book are principles of priority and principles of equality. We can rephrase our task of defending the importance of securing enough as a demand of justice, then, as examining whether some sufficientarian principles are distinctive and more plausible than the most plausible principles of equality and priority. To do so, we can proceed in two stages. First, we should identify what is distinctive about sufficientarian principles. Second, we should determine the plausibility of such principles where distinct from their rivals: equality and priority.

Since only distinctive sufficientarian principles can even hope to be indispensable to a complete and sound account of justice that ought to guide our decisions, my aim in this chapter is to clarify the general structure of distinctive sufficientarian principles in a way that shows that they need not be vulnerable to certain compelling objections that have been made of them. A good place to start identifying the special importance of securing enough is with past examinations of the relative plausibility of sufficientarian principles. This will help us to see what has been thought to be distinctive about the appeal to sufficiency and then we can see whether that is plausible.

Historic Uses of Sufficiency

The notion at the heart of sufficientarian principles of justice is the idea that securing enough is especially important. This special importance has been specified in the form of sufficientarian principles in two main ways, both of which are vulnerable to powerful objections. I summarise both views here and the objections to them before articulating what I take to be the fundamental structure of distinctive sufficientarian principles and showing that they may avoid these objections. This is a crucial way in which much sufficientarian thinking has been mistaken and correcting this sets us on the right course to seeing the indispensable importance of sufficiency as a demand of justice.

Headcount Sufficientarianism

Endorsing what I call *Headcount Sufficientarianism*, some have favoured maximising the number of individuals who secure enough of some good.[3] This position expresses the following claim:

> *The Headcount Claim*: We should maximise the number of people who have at least enough of some good.

Proponents of this view see the special importance of securing enough as consisting in the imperative to maximise the number of people who have secured it. We can see the implications of such a view in Table 2.1. In the table, A, B and C represent different

Table 2.1 Maximizing sufficiency

	I	II	III	IV	V	VI
A	5	3	3	2	2	2
B	5	5	0	0	0	0
C	4	4	4	4	4	4

societies and I–VI represent equally sized groups in society. The numbers in the boxes represent each individual's share of the currency of distributive justice, whatever that is. The sufficiency threshold is 5 and the same for all.

Headcount sufficientarianism ranks options in the following order: B, A, C. Versions of prioritarianism would likely rank the options in the reverse order: C, A, B. Versions of egalitarianism would likely rank the options C, A, B also.

Headcount sufficientarianism provides distinctive guidance in scenarios where we can maximise sufficiency at the expense of benefitting the worse off. Headcount sufficientarian principles are distinctive where we can benefit the better off who can be brought up to the threshold at the expense of benefitting the worse off who are unavoidably below the threshold but can nonetheless be benefitted. Whether versions of headcount sufficientarianism are dispensable or not turns on the plausibility of favouring the better off in such cases.

In ordinary cases we will think that favouring the better off is implausible, which gives us reason to think that headcount sufficientarianism is not an indispensable guiding principle. To illustrate this point consider a threshold of 100 units, where 100 units represents being well off and 1 unit represents being extremely badly off. A version of headcount sufficientarianism will hold that we should benefit a person with 99 units by 1 unit at the expense of benefitting a person with 1 unit by 98 units, but this seems to be the wrong guidance. In this case it seems that we should benefit the very badly off person by 98 units. A practical case that might be a good model is that of those who are not receiving the equivalent of a 'living wage'.[4] We can maximise the number of people who earn a 'living wage' by increasing, by small amounts, the wages of those who earn just less than a 'living wage' rather than by increasing by large amounts the wages of those who earn way below that level. Headcount sufficientarianism recommends the first policy, but it leaves those earning the very least avoidably very badly off in order to improve the wages of the better off, but still not earning the living wage, by a small amount. However high or low we set the threshold, some version of this objection can run. The availability of such counter-examples renders these views relatively implausible since rival principles would favour benefitting the worse off in such cases. So, the guidance offered by these principles is relatively less plausible than the guidance offered by their non-sufficientarian rivals.

However, there is a set of unusual cases in which headcount sufficientarianism has been thought especially plausible. These are so-called *triage cases*. In triage cases some potential recipients of benefits remain below some putatively critical minimum threshold in any of the distributions. Harry Frankfurt and John Roemer use examples of extreme scarcity to illustrate how headcount sufficientarianism can seem to be a uniquely attractive guide.[5] Consider the case illustrated in Table 2.2 where there are ten patients in a hospital each of whom needs five units of medicine to survive and there are only forty units of the medicine available.

'B' is an equal distribution and, assuming that medicine is the appropriate currency, would be favoured by prioritarians and egalitarians. In 'B' ten people die. In 'A' two people die and eight survive. Where survival is at stake, maximising the number of survivors seems to be the most plausible guidance and to the extent that only headcount sufficientarianism can provide this guidance, we should accept it as one of our guiding principles.

However, even in triage cases it seems that other principles can provide us with this guidance too. More plausible prioritarian principles will recognise welfare, not medicine, as the currency of distributive justice. These principles will recommend distribution

Table 2.2 Triage

	I	II	III	IV	V	VI	VII	VIII	IX	X
A	5	5	5	5	5	5	5	5	0	0
B	4	4	4	4	4	4	4	4	4	4

A over distribution B. Assuming that the medicine has only life-saving properties, and not pain-relieving properties, if five units is sufficient for survival, then we can only improve the welfare of two people. Since the alternative is that everyone is equally badly off, some versions of weighted prioritarianism, which claim that we should attach weight to benefitting persons in proportion to how well off they are, recommend that five units in this case amounts to, say, one unit of welfare. Indeed, it is odd to think that medicine is the correct currency of justice. We require medicine insofar as it keeps us healthy and health insofar as it enables us to live well, one could argue. Certainly, if medicine did not improve our health or quality of life, if it were the wrong medicine for instance, we would lack the main reason to care about its distribution. Although getting enough of some good is, in this case, undoubtedly important, we do not need to appeal to sufficientarian principles to get the most plausible guidance. From this, we should conclude that even in triage cases headcount sufficientarian principles are not more plausible guides than their rivals and they do not seem likely to feature in a complete and sound theory of distributive justice.

Excessive Upward Transfers

There is a more systematic way of arguing against headcount sufficientarianism. We can characterise the general objection critics have made in terms of the excessive upward transfers objection:

> *The Excessive Upward Transfers Objection*: Headcount sufficientarian principles are dispensable because they provide distinctive guidance only where they recommend distributing, perhaps tiny, benefits to those closer to the threshold by denying, perhaps massive, benefits to those further below. This is a highly implausible implication that rival views, such as prioritarianism and egalitarianism, can avoid.

All of the cases that distinguish headcount sufficientarianism from prioritarianism are cases of what Dale Dorsey calls 'upward transfers'.[6] They involve benefitting the better off at the expense of the worse off either by transferring benefits from the worse off, upwards, to the better off or by ensuring that the worse off forgo benefits so that the better off can enjoy them. This objection applies in virtue of the headcount claim that is definitive of headcount sufficientarianism. Because of this, these principles are inherently vulnerable to what seems to be a very powerful objection. This provides us with a reason to think that we can and should do without headcount sufficientarian principles in a complete and sound theory of distributive justice. They seem thoroughly dispensable. If some sufficientarian principles do make it into that theory, which will be our guide, it is not likely that they will be headcount sufficientarian principles.

Upper Limit Sufficientarianism

Others have understood the special importance of securing enough as a point beyond which we should not be concerned with how benefits are distributed between people.[7] I call this *Upper Limit Sufficientarianism*.[8] Different versions of upper limit sufficientarianism set the level of sufficiency differently, and defenders of the view disagree about the correct distribution of goods where sufficiency for all is not possible. However, every upper limit sufficientarian accepts what I call the 'upper limit claim':

> *The Upper Limit Claim*: No distributive principles apply to benefits among those who have secured enough.[9]

Upper limit sufficientarianism captures the anti-egalitarian spirit of many sufficientarian principles. These principles typically claim that diminishing weight should apply to those who lack 'enough', and only those who lack enough.[10] Thus, on this view, policies that benefit those who have enough should not be favoured over policies that are otherwise the same but do not benefit those with enough. Using a practical example to illustrate their guidance, we can say that if those who pay the top rate of income tax have *enough* after tax, a policy to cut the top rate of income tax will not make society more just. The fact that those who have already secured enough will benefit does not give us any reason to favour the policy. One could, of course, appeal to additional principles, such as aggregative principles, to express a preference for a cut in

Table 2.3 Upper limit sufficientarianism

	I	II	III	IV	V	VI
A	1,000	1,000	1,000	1,000	1,000	3
B	5	5	5	5	5	5
C	5	5	280	5	5	4

tax at the top rate but so could rival views and as such it is not a distinct advantage of upper limit sufficientarianism that it is able to accommodate those convictions in this way.[11]

Upper limit sufficientarianism provides distinct guidance from prioritarian and egalitarian principles in the situations illustrated in Table 2.3.

Common versions of upper limit sufficientarianism state that we should prefer B to C, where the threshold is 5, and we should prefer B and C to A.[12] Weighted prioritarianism ranks the options A, C, B, in order of most preferred to least preferred. Versions of upper limit sufficientarianism give identical guidance to some forms of prioritarianism in cases involving only those who lack enough. This would be the case if the threshold was at 1,001, for instance. However, in cases involving only those who have secured enough, upper limit sufficientarianism is distinct from prioritarianism. For example, if we can benefit the worse off, and they have secured enough, upper limit sufficientarianism is indifferent about giving priority to the worse off, but each form of prioritarianism is not. This might initially strike us as implausible and lead us to doubt whether upper limit sufficientarian principles, rather than prioritarian principles, should be taken as our guide.

Objectionable Indifference

Upper limit sufficientarian principles are distinct from other principles in virtue of their inability to condemn some regressive policies, which require greater contributions from the worse off than the better off, and are unable to condemn huge inequalities between those who have secured enough.[13] The specific counter-examples that are available to the critics of upper limit sufficientarianism depend on the location of the threshold, but critics have argued convincingly that no matter how high or low the threshold, upper limit sufficientarians will be vulnerable to at least one powerful objection.

The lower that upper limit sufficientarians set the threshold, the more implausible their guidance becomes because their indifference to the distribution of benefits and burdens covers a larger range of well-being scores. If we set the upper limit at a level we are familiar with, perhaps at the level of the quite well off, the indifference would mean that we could not give greater weight to those in society who are quite well off rather than another group in society who are very well off. For example, if the threshold is set at £30,000 or £40,000 annual income and we could help some group who received £50,000 annually or some group who received £900,000 annually, the upper limit sufficientarian would be indifferent about who gets the help. It seems, however, that we should not be indifferent. We should be giving priority to the worse off where we can help either those who are the very well off or those who are merely quite well off. Since prioritarians always favour helping the worse off, they will give us what looks like the most plausible guidance in this case and so upper limit sufficientarianism looks relatively implausible and therefore dispensable to a complete and sound theory of distributive justice.

To avoid this problem upper limit sufficientarians could set the upper limit so high that very few if any individuals ever attained that level, perhaps at the level of £1,000,000,000 annual income.[14] This makes indifference appear more plausible. We do not seem to have reason to care about the inequalities amongst different billionaires, or their welfare equivalents, though these inequalities are *far* greater than the inequalities between those who are less well off that do disturb us.

While raising the upper limit threshold renders indifference less troubling, it also renders this piece of guidance no longer a distinct advantage. If the threshold is very high, the recommendations given by an upper limit sufficientarian principle would fail to be distinctive in just the situations for which we require guidance.[15] Since upper limit sufficientarians usually claim that we should give weighted priority to those below the threshold, they usually provide identical guidance to some form of prioritarianism. The class of cases for which we are most in need of guidance occurs below a high threshold, and we could appeal to another distributive principle below the threshold and get identical guidance to that offered by upper limit sufficientarianism. We can rephrase the description of the circumstances of justice to bring into sharper focus the problem of high upper limit sufficientarianism by changing 'all claims for benefits can be satisfied' to 'there is enough for all claims to be satisfied'.[16] This is exactly the way that upper limit sufficientarians seem to be using the term 'enough' and it renders their view dispensable in debates about justice. Therefore, sufficientarian principles recommending a high upper limit cannot be indispensable because they are not distinctive in terms of their guidance. As such, they appear unlikely to feature in a complete and sound theory of distributive justice.

A New Role for Sufficiency

If upper limit sufficientarian and headcount sufficientarian principles were exhaustive of the sufficientarian principles that can guide our deliberations about distributive justice – an assumption that seems warranted because these principles virtually exhaust the relevant literature – we should conclude that sufficientarian principles are not indispensable to a sound and complete theory of distributive justice. But this is too quick.

Whether sufficientarian principles are indispensable to a sound and complete theory of distributive justice does not depend on whether previously advocated sufficientarian principles give relatively more plausible guidance than their rivals where distinctive, but rather depends on whether any conceivable sufficientarian principles give relatively more plausible guidance than their rivals where distinctive, and this depends on the relative plausibility of what is fundamentally distinctive about sufficientarian principles. In other words: what truth(s) about distributive justice can sufficientarian principles identify that egalitarian and prioritarian principles cannot? To complete our examination, then, we need to specify the fundamental structure of sufficientarian principles; we must identify the minimum claims that sufficientarians must make about the special importance of securing enough in order to offer distinctive guidance. Only by assessing those claims can we see if sufficientarian principles are truly dispensable or indispensable and to what extent they should play a role in our thought about practical debates.

What is Sufficientarianism?

To be indispensable to a sound and complete theory of distributive justice, principles must be distinctive and more plausible than their rivals. To proceed, then, we must carry out two tasks. First, we must identify and clarify the minimum claims sufficientarian principles must make to offer distinctive guidance. This amounts to identifying a claim or set of claims that sufficientarians and only sufficientarians can and must make. Second, we must assess whether these claims will provide more plausible guidance than the claims made by their rivals. This second task has two parts. The first part requires us to establish whether these claims render all sufficientarian principles implausible, for instance, by being vulnerable to the general objections raised to headcount and upper limit sufficientarianism. In this chapter I will show that they are not vulnerable to these objections. The second part requires us to establish whether particular sufficientarian principles are more plausible than particular rival principles. In subsequent chapters I will argue that some sufficientarian principles are more plausible than their rivals with respect to particular debates, and are therefore indispensable to a sound and complete theory of distributive justice and should therefore be used to guide us.

The Structure of Sufficientarianism

Paula Casal attempts to articulate the fundamental claims that specify the structure of sufficientarianism so I begin by noting a number of Casal's contributions and I build upon these.[17] Casal notes that sufficientarians express the positive thesis:

> *Casal's Positive Thesis*: It is important that people live above a certain threshold, free from deprivation.[18]

This claim articulates a key idea of sufficientarianism: that providing people with enough is important. However, this claim requires a few refinements to be considered a necessary claim for any distinctive, and therefore possibly indispensable, sufficientarian principle.

The term 'deprivation' seems to suggest a low threshold but a sufficiency threshold may be high.[19] For instance, Roger Crisp's version of sufficientarianism does not claim that there is a threshold at the point of deprivation in this sense. Crisp's threshold is set by appeal to compassion felt by an impartial spectator.[20] There is no reason to think that only circumstances involving deprivation would elicit compassion from an impartial spectator. We often feel compassion for those who are unlucky in love or those who lose their dog, even if they are rather well off overall. It seems, then, that sufficiency thresholds need not be linked to deprivation.

It should also be noted that sufficientarian principles must claim that we have weighty reasons to secure enough. If securing enough is a less than weighty demand, then sufficientarian principles would be trivial, lightweight principles that do not make a significant difference in any situation for which we require guidance. However, securing enough need not be the weightiest distributive demand for a sufficientarian principle to be indispensable to a complete and sound theory of distributive justice. For example, securing equal civil liberties might be more important than securing sufficient wealth, but once equal civil liberties are secured, the sufficient wealth principle would become operative and will have an important role to play in guiding us.[21]

Sufficientarian principles must also state that securing enough is a non-instrumentally weighty demand. Sufficientarian principles are dispensable if securing enough is *only* important as a means or instrument to meet the demands of other principles. For example, we might favour policies to ensure that people have secured enough of some things – enough education, enough wealth, or enough health are worthy policy goals – but if these policies are grounded in a non-sufficientarian distributive principle, perhaps a prioritarian principle of welfare, there would be no need for sufficientarian principles to account for this guidance.

Reasons that support a sufficientarian principle, though they must be non-instrumentally weighty, need not be fundamentally weighty. Non-instrumental reasons are necessary to establish an indispensable role for a sufficientarian principle. If securing enough of some good is necessary to satisfy the demands of a fundamental reason, then we would have a non-instrumental reason to secure enough. For example, we may have a fundamental reason to establish, say, a society of equals and securing sufficient health might be a fixed demand in such a society. In this case the reason to secure sufficient health would not itself be fundamental, but a sufficientarian distributive principle for health could not be omitted from a complete and sound theory of justice as a society of equals and as such is indispensable to it.

In light of these considerations, I would restate Casal's positive thesis, as a necessary claim of sufficientarian principles, thus:

> *The Positive Thesis*: We have weighty non-instrumental reasons to secure at least enough of some good(s).

The Positive Thesis is Not Enough

While the revised positive thesis is necessarily a part of any sufficientarian principle, it does not render sufficientarian principles distinct from other principles. This is because some prioritarian and aggregative principles claim that we have weighty, non-instrumental reasons to give people more.[22] Advocates of these principles will claim that we have weighty reasons to give people at least the amount that is deemed enough because giving people at least that amount is one way of giving them more, and we always have weighty reasons to give people more. Since we assess the plausibility of principles based on the guidance they would offer, and since the idea of priority can account for this guidance without reference to sufficiency, we reach an impasse where that guidance is identical. Indispensable sufficientarian principles will amount to more than the claim that securing enough is important. Securing enough must somehow be especially important in a way that distinguishes it from these other views in terms of its guidance.

It could be argued that the positive thesis contains the distinctive idea of sufficientarian principles: the sufficiency threshold. However, to provide a full account of the character of distinctive sufficientarian principles we need to explain that idea more explicitly than the positive thesis allows us to.

What is special about the threshold? I propose that sufficiency thresholds mark a change in our weighty, non-instrumental reasons to benefit people. What the sufficiency threshold uniquely allows us to say is that we should treat those who have secured enough differently from those who have not secured enough for the purposes of distributive justice. This seems to fit well with our ordinary use of the terms 'enough' and 'sufficiency'. Once a person has had enough sleep or enough petrol for his or her car, we do not think that there are no further benefits to securing more sleep or petrol, as the upper limit sufficientarian would. Instead, we think that once enough petrol or sleep is secured, our reasons to put more petrol in our cars or to spend more time asleep are changed. In deciding between getting enough petrol and spending money on sweeties we usually have more reason to favour petrol, but once enough petrol is secured, purchasing sweeties is a much more defensible use of our limited resources. Likewise, a choice between returning home early in order to secure enough sleep and staying at the pub for another drink should probably be decided in favour of sleep. But so long as you know you will get enough sleep anyway, perhaps because you have no early appointments the following day, staying out for another drink is a much more defensible decision. A countervailing reason can more easily outweigh our reasons to get more than enough of some good than it can outweigh our reasons to secure just enough of that good. Sufficiency thresholds characterised as a shift or change in our reasons can explain why.

Now, to help establish this claim and the positive thesis as definitive of sufficientarian principles, consider the following examples of intuitively sufficientarian principles of justice that fit this mould. A sufficientarian view may claim that absolute priority applies to benefitting those who have not yet secured enough and that weighted priority applies to further benefits. On this view, we should always benefit those who have less than enough rather than those who have enough. Thus, policies that ensure that people have enough, such as the living wage policy, are to be pursued at the expense of policies that benefit those who already have enough, such as cutting the top rate of income tax. Consider another intuitively sufficientarian view, which states that we should give weighted priority to the worse off below the threshold and that once people have secured enough, we should distribute the currency of justice equally.[23] On this view, we should pursue policies that promote sufficiency and then policies that reduce the difference between rich and poor. Often sufficientarianism has been associated with so-called threshold effects, which tend to emphasise a steep rise or drop in the contribution an additional unit makes to some significant factor. These sorts of views cannot be represented by a single equation either, even though the rate at which the importance of an additional benefit changes is the same before and after the steep drop. What explains all of these views is a change or shift in the weight or kind of reasons that we have to secure additional benefits.

The principles in these examples seem to be sufficientarian principles and they seem so in virtue of the different distributive criteria that apply to those who have secured enough and those who have not. The sufficiency threshold, then, seems to mark a shift in the nature of our reasons to benefit people further. This intuitive thought is formally expressed by what I call the 'shift thesis':

The Shift Thesis: Once people have secured enough, there is a discontinuity in the rate of change of the marginal weight of our reasons to benefit them further.

The shift thesis and the positive thesis together render sufficientarianism distinct from prioritarianism. The difference between sufficientarianism and prioritarianism can be seen in the following way. Some, but not all, prioritarians claim that there is no such shift and that priority to the worse off diminishes at a continuous rate.[24] The recommendations of these prioritarian principles can be represented by a smooth curve or straight line on a graph plotting the relationship between the moral importance of one additional unit of benefit and how well off the recipient is (see Figure 2.1). A shift will disrupt this smooth curve. Indeed, if

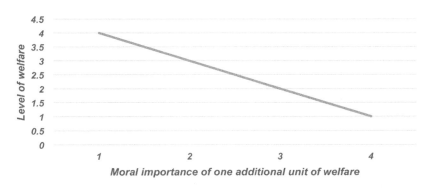

Figure 2.1 Uniform prioritarianism

we should distribute benefits equally once people have secured enough, then we could not plot the guidance entirely on a graph with these axes. As such, sufficientarian principles, so defined, are clearly different from those rival principles.

However, there are other versions of prioritarianism and so it is worth pausing to show that the shift thesis enables sufficientarian principles to offer guidance that is distinct from those principles too. The broadest possible characterisation of prioritarianism states that for equally sized groups A and B, if group A is worse off than group B, then we have weightier reasons to give an equally sized benefit to A than to B. This characterisation of prioritarianism is compatible with the discontinuity that I have called a 'shift' (see Figure 2.2). This characterisation does not contain a commitment to a uniform rate of change in the marginal weight of our reasons to benefit people. This may lead us to think that the shift does not render sufficientarian principles distinct from these views.

Prioritarian views that are compatible with a shift I call 'non-uniform prioritarianism'. Non-uniform prioritarians work out the importance of benefitting those with at least a certain amount of the currency differently than they work out the importance of benefitting those with less than that amount of the currency. To be determinate, non-uniform prioritarian principles must state the different rates at which priority diminishes before and after this shift.

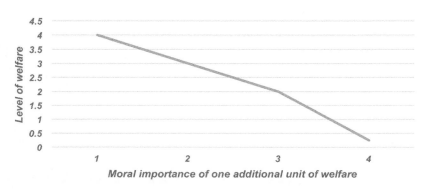

Figure 2.2 Non-uniform prioritarianism

Non-uniform prioritarians cannot explain the shift in terms of merely giving priority to the worse off. Different rates of change are required to explain the change in terms of the relationship between how well off someone is and the moral importance of benefitting them by one additional unit. This change takes place at a welfare level of two in Figure 2.2. The only explanation available to them states that there is a discontinuity in the rate of change of the marginal weight of our reasons to benefit people once they have secured *enough*, which is at a welfare level of two in Figure 2.2. This is just a statement of the shift thesis. In order to account for such a change, then, non-uniform prioritarians must appeal to a sufficientarian principle.[25] They cannot explain the shift in terms of their own notion of giving priority to the worse off. They must reach outside of the concept of priority to explain a feature of their view and to do so they must grasp the concept of sufficiency. These views are prioritarian in the broad sense but a complete theory of justice that is compatible with non-uniform prioritarianism must appeal to at least one sufficientarian principle. This is the distinctive role for sufficientarian principles and it explains the special importance of securing enough as a demand of justice.

Moreover, the role of sufficientarian principles in non-uniform prioritarianism is only one among many possible roles for sufficientarian principles in distributive justice. Shifts are also compatible with views that hold that sufficiency should constrain responsibility-sensitive egalitarianism.[26] Such a view would claim that we should secure enough for everyone but once they have secured enough, inequalities can be justified (only) if they are the result of individuals' choices. Alternatively, a sufficientarian principle could demand that inequalities be to the greatest benefit of the least advantaged, as Rawls's difference principle recommends, and maintain that once everyone has secured enough, benefits should be distributed according to a weighted prioritarian principle.[27] These sufficientarian principles, which explain a shift in our reasons, are distinct from even non-uniform prioritarianism and so there are many different types of distinctive sufficientarian principle.

Together the *positive thesis* and the *shift thesis* comprise the minimum claims of any sufficientarian principle offering distinctive guidance. Articulating these claims together draws our attention to the general structure that sufficientarian principles must have if they are to be indispensable demands of justice.

Upper limit and headcount sufficientarianism are, of course, versions of shift sufficientarianism on a broad characterisation of sufficientarianism. Upper limit sufficientarians claim that there is a shift from some distributive criteria, usually uniformly diminishing weight, and once everyone has secured enough, no distributive criteria apply. This is an extreme shift. Headcount sufficientarians claim that we should maximise the number of people who have secured enough. Once everyone has secured enough, we cannot maximise the number of those who have secured enough further and so some change must take place in the way benefits and burdens should be distributed.[28] This is another kind of extreme shift. But sufficientarians do not need to be extreme to be distinctive because subtler shifts are distinctive.

Avoiding the Objections

Together the *positive thesis* and the *shift thesis* comprise the minimum claims of any sufficientarian principle capable of offering distinctive guidance. They specify the type of guidance that is uniquely given by sufficientarian principles. I will now show why the objections above do not apply to sufficientarianism in virtue

33

of claims sufficientarians must make, but rather only in terms of claims that certain sufficientarians have made.

The indifference objection stated that sufficientarian principles are implausible because they are objectionably indifferent to inequalities once everyone has secured enough. However, shifts are compatible with a wide range of distributive criteria once everyone has secured enough. For example, sufficientarians can favour the pursuit of policies that promote equality for its own sake once everyone has secured enough.[29]

The excessive upward transfers objection stated that sufficientarian principles are implausible because, amongst those below the threshold, they can recommend benefitting the better off by tiny amounts at the expense of large benefits to the worse off. However, sufficientarians can avoid this objection by appealing to the shift and attaching priority to those who fall short of the threshold. For example, the shift means that sufficientarians can claim that the difference principle – which, as standardly understood, holds that we should maximise the position of the least well off – applies to those who have not secured enough.[30] Both of these objections can be avoided.

When is Sufficiency Indispensable?

Whether sufficientarian principles are indispensable depends upon whether they offer more plausible guidance than their rivals where distinctive. What is distinctive about sufficientarian principles is the shift articulated jointly by the shift thesis and the positive thesis. Therefore, to test whether sufficientarian principles are indispensable we need to work out the conditions under which claiming that there is a shift in our reasons is more plausible than denying it. We can specify some of the conditions under which shifts will be plausible by focussing on the claims that the positive thesis and the shift thesis make about reasons.

Recall the positive thesis:

The Positive Thesis: We have weighty non-instrumental reasons to secure at least enough of some good(s).

It follows that for there to be a shift there must be at least one non-instrumental, weighty reason to secure at least enough of some good(s). Now, recall the shift thesis:

The Shift Thesis: Once people have secured enough, there is a discontinuity in the rate of change of the marginal weight of our reasons to benefit them further.

A discontinuity in the rate of change of the marginal weight of our reasons to benefit people further can be explained in the following, non-technical, way. When we are discussing the weight of our reasons to benefit someone, we are discussing the strength of the claim that an individual has to some benefit. The rate of change of the marginal weight of our reasons to benefit someone is the way that the importance of benefitting her alters as she becomes better off, for example, by becoming weaker. If there is no change in the marginal weight of our reasons to benefit her as she becomes better off, the rate of change is 0. If our reasons to benefit someone decline constantly, in proportion to an improvement in her position, as uniform prioritarians claim, then the rate of change may be 1 or else some other fixed value. A discontinuity in the rate of change of the marginal weight of our reasons to benefit someone means that the rate of change itself changes depending on how well off a person is. So the rate of change of the marginal weight of our reasons may be 1 until someone has secured *enough*, then our reasons to benefit them decline at a quicker or slower rate. If our reasons change to favour an equal or more responsibility sensitive distribution, then the rate at which the marginal weight of our reasons to benefit her changes, but not in line with how well off she is. This too is a discontinuity since the rate of change of our reasons to benefit her is non-continuous.

One way of accounting for the discontinuity is by appealing to satiable reasons that cease to apply to benefits once people have secured enough. If some weighty non-instrumental reasons for benefitting people only apply up to a certain point, then the overall profile of reasons we have to benefit people will change after that point. Those who have not secured enough can call on the weight of more and therefore a different profile of reasons than those who have secured enough. Satiable reasons, then, will support a shift, which in turn supports a sufficientarian principle. This also seems to better account for some of our ordinary claims about the concept of sufficiency. Recall the example about petrol and sweeties. Once I have enough petrol, it seems, my reason to get enough petrol no longer applies, though I still have reasons to get more petrol, perhaps. This means that a reason to spend any remaining money on petrol rather than, for example, sweeties, no longer acts to countervail whatever reasons I originally had to get sweeties and thus, *ceteris paribus*, makes it easier for those countervailing reasons to defeat other reasons.

We can also note that to support a shift, and therefore a distinctive sufficientarian principle, these reasons must be non-egalitarian, to be distinct from egalitarian principles, and sated at a low enough level to provide us with some guidance for real situations, to avoid the high threshold problem. I will now clarify each of the features that reasons must have to support a shift in order to give us a clear idea of this way of testing the prospects for sufficientarianism.[31]

Satiability

In defining satiability, I follow Joseph Raz who does so in the following way:

> Satiable principles are marked by one feature: the demands the principles impose can be completely met. When they are completely met then whatever may happen and whatever might have happened the principles cannot be, nor could they have been, satisfied to a higher degree.[32]

Satiable reasons behave like satiable principles. Satiable reasons are familiar from ordinary discussion. Once a person has secured enough money for a bus ticket, 'for a bus ticket' is no longer a reason to give her more money. Our reasons to benefit people change when they are no longer deficient in the relevant respect. There may be strong claims for benefits beyond the application of that reason, we need not be upper limit sufficientarians, but such claims must be made using a different profile of reasons. This alters our all things considered reasons to benefit people further.

Avoid a High Threshold

In order to offer distinctive guidance, sufficientarian principles can be supported by satiable reasons, but these satiable reasons cannot be stated at a point that is so high they would set a very high threshold. If a sufficientarian principle has a high threshold, then its guidance will be identical to the guidance provided by the distributive criteria that apply prior to the shift in realistic circumstances. We might say that the reason must be sated within moderate scarcity where benefits are neither extremely scarce, such that no competing claims can be met, nor superabundant, such that all claims can be met.[33]

Non-instrumental

To support a shift that reason must also be non-instrumentally weighty. As I discussed when clarifying the positive thesis, if securing enough is important only because securing enough serves some other distributive principle, like principles of priority or equality, then we can account for the shift without reference to a sufficientarian principle. As such, instrumental reasons cannot support an indispensable sufficientarian principle.

Reasons supporting a shift need not be fundamentally weighty, however. Non-instrumental reasons are sufficient to establish an indispensable role for a sufficientarian principle. If securing enough of something is necessary to satisfy the demands of a fundamental reason, then we would have a non-instrumental reason to secure enough. We may have a fundamental reason to establish, say, a society of equals of which sufficient health might be a fixed part. In this case the reason to secure enough health would not itself be fundamental, but the sufficientarian principle it supported could not be omitted from a complete and sound theory of distributive justice.

A special case of instrumental is worth discussing. The reasons we have to secure enough must not be sated only by an exactly equal distribution of the good in question. If enough just meant enough for equality, then the sufficientarian principle would not be distinct from some principles of equality because it would be instrumental to the equality principle. On some understandings distributive equality is not a satiable demand, as discussed in Chapter 1. However, equality can be understood as a satiable demand. I have called these views simple equality, and so I have stressed that satiable egalitarian reasons cannot support a sufficientarian shift.

This highlights the forms of egalitarianism with which sufficientarian principles are incompatible: those that advocate levelling down to levels below the threshold. Sufficientarian principles are incompatible with egalitarian principles, which claim that all that is required is exactly equal shares of benefits, but are compatible with egalitarian ideals like the ideal of a society of equals or some egalitarian principles that claim we should secure equality only once we have secured sufficiency. Rivalry with equality in all its guises is not essential to the sufficientarian position because part of showing equal concern could be to give special priority to benefitting those who have not secured enough.

Weighty

Finally, to support a shift the reason to secure enough must also be weighty. If securing enough is not a weighty demand, the sufficientarian principle it supports would be a trivial, lightweight consideration that does not make a significant difference to the overall guidance. However, securing enough need not be the weightiest distributive demand for the sufficientarian principle it supports to be indispensable. In order to support distinctive sufficientarian principles, these reasons must be weightier than trivial but need not be the weightiest reasons we have.

Summary

I shall term reasons that meet all of the above criteria 'sufficientarian reasons'. Sufficientarian principles supported by these reasons will be indispensable and so if, in some debates about justice, we have sufficientarian reasons, then sufficientarian principles will have an indispensable role in a complete and sound theory of distributive justice.

It remains for me to show that we have such reasons and that the principles they support are more plausible than those of their rivals. However, we should also note another way to explain shifts in the weight of our reasons to confer goods on persons once they have secured enough. This method emphasises changes in the importance of securing more of some good relative to some other good. I call this the 'value clash argument'. The intuitive idea behind this line of argument is that where one value clashes with another, and both seem somewhat indispensable, the best principle to adhere to in adjudicating which to promote may be a principle that states that the weight of our reasons to advance one value shifts once the other value has been promoted to a sufficient extent. For example, if value A and value B seem relevant to some set of decisions and we cannot promote both, it may be best to follow the principle that states that we should promote A to a sufficient extent and then promote B. This may be because A is initially a greater value but diminishes in its importance. When enough is secured, the value of promoting A has diminished sufficiently to make advances in B more important. Thus, the relative importance of securing B changes once enough of A is secured. This is an alternative to dismissing one of the values or of giving lexical priority to one value. If, as I will claim, some value clashes are most plausibly resolved by sufficientarian principles, then it seems we should be optimistic about the prospects for sufficientarianism insofar as there are such clashes.

Conclusion

Historically, sufficiency, as a demand of justice, has been understood in two ways and each of these is vulnerable to powerful objections. However, distinctive sufficientarian principles can avoid these objections. I have provided a clarification of the special importance that sufficiency has as a claim of justice. This special importance is best articulated by two claims, the shift thesis and the positive thesis. Together these two claims hold that securing enough is a weighty, non-instrumental demand of justice and that once people have secured enough, our reasons to benefit them shift such that there is a discontinuity in the marginal weight of our reasons to benefit them further.

I described how sufficientarian reasons can support a shift. I argued that if some of our reasons to benefit people with respect to some goods are satiable, weighty and non-instrumental, then we would have a shift that can only be accounted for by an indispensable sufficientarian principle. In subsequent chapters of this book I will use this line of argument to defend an indispensable sufficientarian principle and will then show that this principle has important implications and should play an extensive role in our thought. In other chapters of this book I will use the value clash line of argument to defend an indispensable sufficientarian principle and show that it has important practical implications and should have an extensive role in our thought. This book as a whole seeks not only to vindicate the claim that the prospects for sufficientarianism are better than has been thought, but also to vindicate these two lines of argument for defending and identifying sufficientarian principles.

Notes

1. This chapter is derived, in part, from Shields, 'The prospects for sufficientarianism'.
2. For some objections that I have not considered, because they are aimed at specific telic versions of sufficientarianism, see Segall, 'What is the point of sufficiency?' For a response, see Nielsen, 'Sufficiency grounded as sufficiently free'.
3. Arneson, 'Distributive justice and basic capability equality', 26–33, 36–8; Benbaji, 'The doctrine of sufficiency: a defence', 311; Casal, 'Why sufficiency is not enough', 298, 315–16; Dorsey, 'Toward a theory of the basic minimum'; Page, *Climate Change, Justice and Future Generations*, 85–95; Page, 'Justice between generations', 11; Roemer, 'Eclectic distributional ethics', 273–4, 278–9.
4. The idea of a living wage is to meet a certain cost of living deemed to be minimally decent. For more, see <http://www.livingwage.org. uk/> (last accessed 24 March 2016).

5. Frankfurt, 'Equality as a moral ideal', 31; Roemer, 'Eclectic distributional ethics', 273–4.
6. Dorsey, 'Toward a theory of the basic minimum', 432.
7. Frankfurt, 'Equality as a moral ideal', 21.
8. Benbaji, 'The doctrine of sufficiency'; Benbaji, 'Sufficiency or priority?'; Brighouse and Swift, 'Educational equality versus educational adequacy', 125–6; Casal, 'Why sufficiency is not enough', 298–300, 310–14; Crisp, 'Equality, priority, and compassion'; Crisp, 'Egalitarianism and compassion'; Holtug, 'Prioritarianism', 149–54; Huseby, 'Sufficiency'; Kekes, 'A question for egalitarians'; Temkin, 'Equality, priority or what?', 65–6; Temkin, 'Egalitarianism defended'; Widerquist, 'How the sufficiency minimum becomes a social maximum'. In Axelsen and Nielsen, 'Sufficiency as freedom from duress', the authors advance a form of upper limit sufficientarianism but are pluralist about the currency, which enables them to respond to the indifference objection.
9. This is similar to what Casal calls the 'negative thesis' in 'Why sufficiency is not enough', 289.
10. Crisp, 'Equality, priority, and compassion', 758; Huseby, 'Sufficiency'.
11. Roger Crisp suggests that utilitarianism above the threshold is a plausible view in Crisp, 'Equality, priority, and compassion', 758.
12. Benbaji, 'Doctrine of sufficiency', 312; Crisp, 'Equality, priority, and compassion', 758.
13. Arneson, 'Distributive justice and basic capability equality', 36–8; Benbaji, 'Doctrine of sufficiency'; Benbaji, 'Sufficiency or priority?'; Brighouse and Swift, 'Educational equality versus educational adequacy', 125–6; Casal, 'Why sufficiency is not enough', 298–300, 310–14; Crisp, 'Equality, priority, and compassion'; Crisp, 'Egalitarianism and compassion'; Frankfurt, 'Equality as a moral ideal'; Holtug, 'Prioritarianism', 149–54; Huseby, 'Sufficiency', 190; Temkin, 'Equality, priority or what?', 65–6; Temkin, 'Egalitarianism defended', 765–6, 769–76.
14. Crisp, 'Equality, priority, and compassion'; Crisp, 'Egalitarianism and compassion'; Frankfurt, 'Equality as a moral ideal'; Huseby, 'Sufficiency'.
15. Casal, 'Why sufficiency is not enough', 317–18.
16. Rawls, *A Theory of Justice*, 109–12.
17. Casal, 'Why sufficiency is not enough'.
18. In Casal, 'Why sufficiency is not enough', 298–9, the author claims

that 'The positive thesis stresses the importance of people living above a certain threshold, free from deprivation.'

19. Anderson, 'Fair opportunity in education', 596; Casal, 'Why sufficiency is not enough', 321–3; Crisp, 'Equality, priority, and compassion', 755–63; Satz, 'Equality, adequacy, and education for citizenship', 636–9.

20. In Crisp, 'Equality, priority, and compassion', 757, the author states that 'The notion of compassion, then, used in conjunction with the notion of an impartial spectator, may provide us with the materials for an account of distribution which allows us to give priority to those who are worse off when, and only when, these worse off are themselves badly off.'

21. In Rawls, *Justice as Fairness*, 44 n.7, the author states that 'This principle (the liberty principle) may be preceded by a lexically prior principle requiring that basic needs be met, as [sic] least insofar as their being met is a necessary condition for citizens to understand and to be able fruitfully to exercise the basic rights and liberties.'

22. Arneson, 'Perfectionism and politics', 57; Arneson, 'Welfare should be the currency of justice'; Holtug, 'Prioritarianism', 132–3; Parfit, 'Equality or priority?', 100–1.

23. Williams, 'Liberty, equality, and property'.

24. Hirose, 'Reconsidering the value of equality'; Holtug, 'Prioritarianism', 134; Peterson and Ove Hansson, 'Equality and priority', 301; Weirlich, 'Utility tempered with equality', 431–3. For criticism of prioritarians who do not provide a principled explanation of the discount rate for benefits, see Orr, 'Sufficiency of resources and political morality'; Williams, 'Equality, ambition, and insurance', 135.

25. Brown, 'Priority or sufficiency . . . or both?'

26. Casal, 'Why sufficiency is not enough', 321–3; Williams, 'Liberty, equality, and property', 501–3.

27. Rawls, *Justice as Fairness*, 42–3.

28. Headcount sufficientarianism would not be satiable if we take it to apply to population numbers. For instance, we could try to maximise the number of people who have secured enough by increasing the population. For population ethics as a problem for headcount sufficientarians, see Casal, 'Why sufficiency is not enough', 298–9.

29. For a discussion of this objection and a defence of upper limit sufficientarianism against it, see Kanschik, 'Why sufficientarianism is not indifferent to taxation'.

30. Rawls, *A Theory of Justice*, 53.

31. I am very grateful to an anonymous reviewer at *Utilitas* for suggesting that I explain these features in this way.
32. Raz, *The Morality of Freedom*, 235–6.
33. Rawls, *A Theory of Justice*, 109–12.

3 The Principle of Sufficient Autonomy

In the last chapter I argued that we should re-examine the prospects for sufficientarianism because once we have clarified the two claims that comprise the structure of sufficientarian principles, we see that they can avoid the objections that have brought them into disrepute. In this chapter I begin that re-examination by arguing for a principle of sufficient autonomy, but before I begin it is worth restating what is meant by the prospects for sufficientarianism.

The prospects for sufficientarianism are a function of two factors: (1) the indispensability of specific sufficiency principles; and (2) the extent of the role those principles should play in our thought about practical debates. Our first task in examining the prospects for sufficientarianism is to see if there are any indispensable sufficientarian principles. Only then can we ask how many there are and the extent of the role each should play in our thought about practical debates.

In the final part of Chapter 2, I discussed two ways of testing whether it is plausible to think that there is a shift and thus, whether there are any indispensable sufficientarian principles in a complete and sound theory of distributive justice. In explaining this first line of argument I claimed that the positive thesis and the shift thesis, taken together, make claims about the kinds of reasons that we have, and that the shift thesis and the positive thesis can be explained by appealing to reasons that are non-instrumental, non-egalitarian, weighty and satiable. These reasons I have called 'sufficientarian reasons'. Sufficientarian reasons support a shift because if some of our reasons to benefit people are of this kind, then once that reason has been sated, our overall profile of reasons to benefit people will change.

In this chapter I will explore this line of argument and, in particular, I will use it to defend a principle of sufficient autonomy as indispensable. In Chapter 4 I show that this principle should have an extensive role in our thought, particularly with respect to practical debates about schooling, and thus show that the second factor that influences the prospects for sufficientarianism is enhanced.

Introduction

The sufficientarian reason that I will defend in this chapter is the reason we have to form beliefs about the good life under the conditions of freedom. My argument will be that sufficient autonomy, understood as a deliberative capacity, constitutes part of the conditions of freedom, and thus, we have a reason to provide people with sufficient autonomy that does not apply to promoting autonomy further. This sufficientarian reason causes a shift in our reasons to promote autonomy once people have secured enough and thus supports a sufficientarian principle. This is entirely consistent with there being further reasons to promote autonomy, albeit reasons of a different sort. The overall aim is to defend a non-instrumental principle of sufficient autonomy as a demand of justice and thereby support the prospects for sufficientarianism. Although this aim requires certain claims about the nature and value of autonomy to be true, this chapter does not attempt to defend a novel account of autonomy as a demand of justice. Rather, it aims to show that we have a sufficientarian reason to promote a type of autonomy that we have reason to value on many different accounts of justice.

Since my aim is to defend the conditions of freedom as providing us with a sufficientarian reason to promote autonomy, and since sufficientarian reasons are weighty, non-instrumental, non-egalitarian and satiable, I shall proceed as follows.

To begin, I will motivate our interest in autonomy as a demand of justice that requires a sufficientarian principle. I begin by showing that autonomy is linked to injustices and for that reason a complete and sound theory of justice must be able to account for these injuries. I shall then show that we can have more or less autonomy and this means that we should be concerned with how far our reasons support promoting autonomy across different persons. This enables us to ask whether autonomy may be a sufficientarian demand of distributive justice because it is a demand of justice and requires a principle of distribution to tell us how it should be promoted.

Next, I set out and provide an initial defence of the account of autonomy that constitutes the conditions of freedom. I also show that alternative sufficientarian reasons would not help to provide the strongest defence of a principle of sufficient autonomy.

Then, I defend the existence of a shift and the indispensability of a principle of sufficient autonomy by showing that the alternative positions are relatively implausible. This is achieved in two parts. In the first part of the section, I show that maximising or prioritising views of autonomy are unable to explain key convictions that underpin our initial concern with autonomy. In the second part of the section, I reject the view that any special concern with securing sufficient autonomy can be captured by an instrumental principle and so the presence of this instrumental shift does not ground an indispensable sufficientarian principle. This leads me to conclude that a sufficientarian principle of autonomy is relatively more plausible than rival views and as such is indispensable to a complete and sound theory of distributive justice.

Following this chapter, in the next, I show why this principle of sufficient autonomy should be given an extensive role in our thought about practical debates about educational provision.

Autonomy

The aim of this section is to establish that securing some level of autonomy is a weighty demand of distributive justice. To this end, I carry out three tasks. First of all, I provide a sketch of autonomy to fix ideas. Second, I show that autonomy is a concern of justice. Third, I show that we can have more or less of it by identifying some violations of autonomy as injustices to show that autonomy is a concern of distributive justice. That autonomy is a concern of justice, and that we can have more or less of it, establishes that the question 'How should autonomy be promoted?' is an important question for distributive justice. This means that we need some principle of justice that can account for our intuitions about the importance of autonomy and how it should be promoted and protected.

What is Autonomy?

Autonomy is the ideal of living one's life in accordance with one's own authentic judgements. Autonomous individuals' lives are directed by themselves and not by others.[1] There are many different notions of autonomy as an ideal, and there is disagreement about the most appropriate way to characterise its nature and its value for the purposes of a theory of distributive justice. Theorists disagree about the importance of autonomy relative to other values, and they disagree about the role of options, powers of planning and the role of rationality within the most appropriate conception of autonomy for any given question.[2] However, any acceptable account of autonomy will include reference to some core idea of critical deliberation about the direction of one's actions. Such a concern can be found, in one way or another, in many of the most prominent theories of justice.

One of the means by which we can clarify autonomy and its importance is to consider the ways it can be adversely affected. Our autonomy can be adversely affected to the extent that we are unable to direct ourselves in one of two ways. First, one's autonomy is adversely affected to the extent that one is coerced against one's will. Think here, for example, of the mugger who insists that you give him the contents of your wallet by making a credible threat that he will otherwise kill you. One of the things we think is wrong about such a case is that your choice is determined for you by someone else. Even if you would be quite happy to give away the contents of your wallet, you cannot choose otherwise because of the acts of another agent. Second, one may fail to be autonomous by failing to be authentic. Think, for example, of a case where a person is brainwashed into thinking that she should give up the contents of her wallet whenever asked in a threatening voice. Here, when the mugger arrives, she does not give him the wallet or its contents begrudgingly, she gives it to him happily, but her autonomy is adversely affected because the brainwashing has removed her ability to decide for herself. What is thought to be wrong in this case is that the agent is not self-directing because the beliefs or desires that lead her to give up the contents of her wallet, with a smile on her face, are not her own, they are the result of some external force acting upon her beliefs and indirectly her actions. She cannot decide or act otherwise. Her capacity for self-rule and autonomy is circumvented. In both types of case, something strikes us as wrong or problematic, and to explain why will require invoking a commitment to autonomy.

While one's autonomy can be diminished in these ways, one can also enhance one's autonomy in ways that we might think are worthy of promotion for justice. We might think that having certain deliberative powers and argumentative competencies promotes our autonomy. The scope of control we have over aspects of our life can affect the level of autonomy individuals possess since it affects their ability to govern themselves. The scope of control we have, and the number and quality of options available, are social conditions that support autonomy, and as such they affect how much autonomy we may exercise.

I am keen not to develop too specific a view of autonomy here as the kind of autonomy we require for justice can be further specified by appeal to the specific reasons we have to care about it. Just as fishing solely for fun and fishing solely to feed one's family may require different locations and perhaps different tools, so the specific kind of autonomy we should promote will alter in accordance with the kind of autonomy we have reason to promote. This sketch of autonomy is necessary to fix ideas and, in the rest of this section I show that autonomy is a concern of justice and that we should be concerned about its distribution.

Autonomy and Justice

Autonomy places demands on the design of public policy, laws and the basic structure of society generally as well as the conduct of individuals as citizens, and so has implications for political action. That autonomy has such implications is a necessary condition for focussing on the distribution of that good for the purposes of justice. However, this does not imply that autonomy should have its own principle of justice. It merely implies that some principle of justice must capture our intuitive concern with autonomy.

The importance of autonomy as a demand of justice is sometimes thought of as demanding toleration of a variety of ways of life and that basic rights and liberties are protected.[3] These are clear examples of how autonomy has been thought to demand that institutions are designed in a certain way that responds to autonomy. Moreover, injustices sometimes involve infringements of autonomy. Denying a person the space to choose and to carry out his or her choice is a characteristic exhibited by many examples of injustice. For instance, arbitrary arrest prevents us from pursuing a number of our chosen ends; religious or racial persecution and slavery also involve violations of autonomy and are instances of injustice. Moreover, persons can be taken to act less autonomously if social institutions, which typically have a great influence on them, do not successfully diminish certain forms of coercion and deception more subtle than arbitrary arrest. Attempts to regulate the background against which we form the beliefs that typically motivate our actions can help to promote autonomy. If someone is denied information about the likely effects of a medical treatment or if home buyers are denied information about the likely effects of living near a nuclear power station, the decisions they make will be less autonomous than they might have been. Of course, we may find that all of the injustices that involve violations of autonomy can be accounted for by the instrumental importance of autonomy but, whatever the truth of that claim, it is clear that diminished autonomy can constitute an injustice and therefore we require a principle of justice to capture our concern with it.

Degrees of Autonomy

Autonomy is a matter of degree. We can have more or less of it. We can choose policies that successfully promote our ability to self-rule in various ways and to different extents. In terms of justice, then, we should be concerned with the distribution of autonomy. Two dimensions along which the amount of autonomy an agent has are the agent's powers of deliberation and the scope of the decisions over which he or she decides. An agent has more autonomy if she has a wider scope of choice or if she has greater deliberative powers and so inequalities and insufficiencies in autonomy, and also sub-maximal distributions, are possible. For example, those who live in a society that affords them a comprehensive scheme of basic liberties and rights and which encourages critical deliberation about the good life will be more autonomous than those living in societies without each or all of these features, other things being equal. For these reasons, then, the question of how much autonomy people should have is an important one for those concerned with justice. This means that we need a principle of distributive justice that explains how autonomy should be distributed across different persons, and one candidate is sufficiency.

The Principle of Sufficient Autonomy

In this section I will articulate the principle of sufficient autonomy by appealing to the sufficientarian reason we have to live under the conditions of freedom. The social conditions of freedom are the problem to which the principle of sufficient autonomy is the solution. I will then defend this account as more plausible than alternative principles of sufficient autonomy. To this end I explain what I mean by the conditions of freedom and the kind of autonomy supported by them.

Sufficientarian reasons are satiable, weighty, non-egalitarian demands relevant to justice that do not derive their weight from more fundamental reasons. Examining the literature, we can attempt to derive sufficientarian reasons from certain treatments of autonomy. John Rawls claims that we have an interest in the *adequate* development of our two moral powers and that principles of justice must be informed by our highest-order interest in autonomy.[4] Joseph Raz claims that our interest in freedom supports autonomy.[5] Ronald Dworkin states that we have an interest in autonomy since it plays an essential role in the formation and maintenance of authentic personalities, without which we cannot be treated as equals.[6] Gerald Dworkin claims that developing sufficient autonomy is intrinsically valuable as it is a requirement of respect.[7]

My concern when specifying the principle of sufficient autonomy is the conditions of belief formation. These are the conditions under which we should form, and possibly revise, beliefs about the good life that inform our own life plans. Clearly, some conditions can taint our beliefs about the good life. For example, if the prevailing social norms in our society hold that a woman's place is in the home, bearing and raising children, this casts doubt on the authenticity of the beliefs people will hold about the role of women in such a society, especially if they overwhelmingly believe that their place is within the home. Indeed, when we are denied information pertinent to a decision we are making, or are denied adequate time to reflect on the facts, we are often resentful of those who deny us it. For example, consider the boss who tells his employee that she must take a pay cut or else lose her job and also claims that by the time the employee consults her union it will be too late. We do object to being denied the opportunity to deliberate about our actions. The employee may, given the time, decide that she must take the pay cut for her long-term security, or for some other reason, and yet being denied the opportunity to reflect upon it seems to diminish her autonomy too much. If institutions are not designed to limit this, they are unjust.

We do well here to notice that our concern with autonomy may be accounted for by a principle that does not give non-instrumental importance to the conditions of freedom. For instance, a utilitarian view will hold that we should form our beliefs under conditions that are likely to maximise aggregate utility, but I will argue that these views, views that deny that there is a non-instrumental shift in our reasons to promote autonomy, are less plausible than the principle of sufficient autonomy.

To suggest why it is that the non-instrumental approach is promising, consider the following distinction. Citizens have an interest in how well their lives will go and how their determinate conceptions of the good can be further advanced, their preferences satisfied and their ambitions pursued. The main problem of distributive justice is usually understood as distributing all-purpose means or being directly concerned with satisfying citizens' preferences.[8] While justice no doubt demands that the social conditions people live in are conducive to a wide range of conceptions of the good life and accounts of well-being, I will argue that there is an independent interest that citizens have in the conditions under which their ambitions, preferences and other beliefs about what is worth pursuing are formed and revised. Citizens have an interest in forming and holding the beliefs that typically motivate their actions under conditions of freedom. I think this distinction helps motivate a broad base of appeal for the social conditions for freedom since even those primarily concerned with ambitions or preference satisfaction should be concerned with the conditions under which they come about.

The interest we have in the conditions of freedom is well explained by John Rawls, who claims that we have a highest-order interest in the conditions under which our more particular convictions about the good life are formed, pursued and revised.[9] We have a highest-order interest in living a complete life under the social conditions of freedom because only under those conditions can we express our nature and secure our status as free and equal moral persons.[10] Free and equal moral persons have two latent moral powers and, for Rawls at least, the conditions of freedom are constituted by conditions compatible with their adequate development and free and informed exercise.[11]

I will argue that a plausible account of such conditions will not only require that basic liberties are secured, but also require that we are well informed about the decisions relevant to us and the costs of such decisions. The importance of achieving some level of autonomy can be illustrated by the following example. There are risks to moving into a particular house or flat. Imagine that one house is cheaper than many of the other houses you have looked at, but it falls short with respect to some criterion you take to be important. Perhaps it is likely that the house will flood in the next ten years. To get a better idea of the likelihood of flooding you have to consult a surveyor. If you do not know how to, or that you can, consult a surveyor, or if you have false beliefs about the costs of employing a surveyor and believe it beyond your financial reach, you cannot freely decide whether the cheapness of the house makes it a bargain or if the risk of flooding makes its purchase foolish. If we do not know the risk, but we know how to find out about it, we might think that we choose freely, and a social background that enables us to make such decisions freely is an important part of justice. If we are well informed enough to become well informed about the other relevant decisions we make, then our reasons to become more and more well informed thereafter may be very different.

The conditions of freedom require that we are given a certain kind of training in reasoning and that we are encouraged, and given adequate time, to make adjustments and deliberate with others about the good. The social conditions sufficient for this would require a certain kind of education, a tolerant ethos and access to reliable sources of information about the costs of courses of action and about what is possible for us. For example, children must be given an education that allows them to discover and develop their interests and talents. Only when people are given a good chance to know what they might like and what they might be good at, as children, can they be confident that they arrive at their convictions freely.

Our concern is that certain social conditions influence the beliefs we form and we do not always form them freely. The principle of sufficient autonomy, supported by the sufficientarian reason we have to live under the social conditions of freedom, can be stated thus: we have weighty, non-instrumental, non-egalitarian reasons to secure sufficient autonomy to secure the social conditions of freedom. The conditions of freedom are those conditions under which one's beliefs and actions can be considered freely taken. To flesh this out we can say that sufficient autonomy has three conditions. One has secured *sufficient autonomy* when (1) one is well-informed, (2) one can give reasons for one's views, and (3) one has a disposition to exchange reasons and participate in a public deliberative process with others.

It is possible that a suitably thick notion of autonomy alone could account for our intuitions about the social conditions of freedom. Such a thick notion of autonomy might focus on the quality and number of options as well as deliberative and planning competency, but it is unlikely that this will exhaust our reasons to promote autonomy further, especially if we think that autonomy is diminished by certain material or status inequalities, a certain kind of ethos or a lack of certain rights and liberties.[12] Our reasons to have further autonomy are different and further autonomy should be distributed in accordance with different reasons, perhaps those of preference or well-being. I shall make this suggestion about the value of supra-sufficient autonomy throughout, but I do so only to bring into sharper focus a particular shift. My argument does not depend on this suggestion's being sound, but the clarity of exposition may rely on entertaining the thought.

An Ambiguity in Rawls

I have said that Rawls's notion of the social conditions of freedom is a plausible candidate for the sufficientarian reason supporting autonomy, but this brings me to an ambiguity in Rawls's own articulation of these conditions. This ambiguity highlights the role of the principle of sufficient autonomy within the conditions of freedom that I wish to defend. The view of the social conditions of freedom that I defend is more plausible, I will claim, than the view Rawls seems to hold.

We can interpret Rawls's discussions of the social conditions of freedom in one of two ways. Rawls could be understood as claiming that justice requires that we bring about the social conditions that will actually develop our powers of autonomy to a sufficient extent. On this view, the social conditions are met if and only if development of sufficient autonomy is realised within a society. Alternatively, Rawls can be understood as claiming that justice requires only that those social conditions compatible with the development of sufficient autonomy be realised. On this view, the social conditions are met if and only if development of sufficient autonomy is an option in that society.

Rawls seems to support the latter interpretation but I intend to show that the former view is more plausible and thus, that achieving sufficient autonomy, and not merely being able to achieve sufficient autonomy, must be included within the social conditions of freedom.

Referring to the priority of the basic liberties, Rawls states: 'These liberties and their priority are to guarantee equally for all citizens the social conditions essential for the adequate development and the full and informed exercise of these powers in what I shall call "the two fundamental cases".'[13] Here 'essential' can be understood as a necessary condition *for the development of these powers*. This is suggested by the following quote from Rawls about determining the liberties that are to be given priority:

> We consider what liberties provide the political and social conditions essential for the adequate development and full exercise of the two moral powers of free and equal persons. Following this we say: first, that the equal political liberties and of thought enable citizens to develop and to exercise these powers judging the justice of the basic structure of society and its social policies; and second, that liberty of conscience and freedom of association enable citizens to develop and exercise their moral powers in forming and revising and in rationally pursuing (individually or, more often, in association with others) their conceptions of the good.[14]

It seems that the social conditions that Rawls believes should be secured are understood as necessary rather than sufficient conditions for the development and exercise of autonomy that partly constitutes the conditions of freedom, such as the political liberties and other basic liberties. Understood in this way, the interest we have in the conditions of freedom does not support the achievement of sufficient autonomy but merely putting the development of at least sufficient autonomy amongst the options that are available for selection. Thus, the conditions of freedom, on this reading, are just those social conditions in which one *can* be free if one happens to develop and exercise that autonomy. However, if persons have a highest-order interest in being free from natural and social contingency, as Rawls claims, and determining their own path in life, then some level of autonomy must actually be achieved alongside the arrangement of society's basic institutions and not merely be made possible. Sufficient autonomy must be realised.[15]

We must attach far greater urgency to the goal of giving people sufficient autonomy than further improvements. Without achieving the sufficient level of autonomy, even in conditions where its achievement is possible or even likely, one cannot have assurance that one has freely examined what to believe and it would fail some people. It is not as if one is free to choose to develop autonomy in the first place from a non-autonomous starting position. You are not free to leave prison if you *could* break out, or free to enter your home if you *could* find the keys. Someone who does not understand Spanish and can only come to understand that language by following instructions in Spanish is, likewise, not free to learn Spanish. Sufficient autonomy for free belief formation and free choice is what I mean by sufficient autonomy and it is the level of autonomy required to break this cycle.

If, as Rawls seems to state, justice demands that we are merely in a position where we could choose to develop our autonomy, then the decision to do so is determined by social contingency and not our own free choice and so, then, are our life plans. Some level of autonomy is a prerequisite for making free choices, and, as such, there is no *ex ante* position from which persons can freely choose to develop sufficient autonomy. Only once an agent is autonomous can we fully respect his or her answer to the question 'Do you want to enhance your autonomy?' We owe them autonomy sufficient for making these kinds of choices freely as part of justice. Even with basic liberties and other social institutions we cannot be considered free without the achievement of sufficient autonomy.

Having clarified the conditions of freedom required for belief formation and the principle of sufficient autonomy that addresses the problem, I will now elaborate the content of the principle of sufficient autonomy and survey some rival sufficientarian reasons that could ground an alternative principle of sufficient autonomy.

The Significance of Sufficient Autonomy

One reason for promoting individual autonomy is our interest in the conditions of freedom. It is a weighty, non-egalitarian reason that is satiable with respect to autonomy, at least. That is, it requires some autonomy but not maximum autonomy and it is non-instrumentally valuable. The conditions of freedom include a certain kind of training as well as the legal and social possibility of changing our views within some range. Autonomy must be developed to a certain extent if we are to be considered free. While the conditions of freedom may require a certain level of material equality and the eradication of certain social norms, the conditions of freedom also require a level of deliberative power and one must use that deliberative power. Thus, the conditions of freedom require that one must be able to give reasons for one's current view and be capable and willing to deliberate with others. Only when one has these skills and this disposition can one be assured one's views continue to be freely held.

Beyond this must we have better and better deliberative powers? Must we have more and more options? Once we have secured sufficient autonomy, our claims to greater powers of deliberation must be made on different grounds. We need not, and should not, be upper limit sufficientarians about autonomy. Autonomy seems to have some further value insofar as it constitutes a prerequisite for some reasonable ambitions that constitute part of a person's conception of the good. This causes a shift in the way that autonomy ought to be distributed once people have secured enough of it.[16] As long as our choice to further develop those powers would be considered free, then we are already sufficiently autonomous. Our ability and disposition to deliberate with others ensures a way out. The interest, then, is satiable.

We could specify a principle of sufficient autonomy in different ways and some thinkers have suggested how we might do this. I will consider why these ways of specifying sufficient autonomy are less plausible as indispensable sufficientarian principles than the view I have articulated so far. Before doing so I will respond to the claim that the conditions of freedom only matter for some theories of justice that take preferences or responsibility seriously when working out distributive shares.

We might think that theorists like Ronald Dworkin, who refer to ambitions when determining justice, or those who take preference satisfaction as the currency of justice, are under a greater burden than other political philosophers to secure a suitable social background against which those preferences and ambitions are formed.[17] Thus, one may think that the point I am making is a narrow one and only applies to some theories of justice and not others. It might be thought that this would be an important objection to my defence of autonomy as part of the conditions of freedom if there are decisive arguments against these theories. However, I do not think taking our beliefs seriously in this way affects the point I want to make. Whether we think preferences are the currency of justice or that our ambitions and beliefs affect our entitlements, the ability of people to form preferences and conceptions of the good freely is so important that we should care about the social conditions in which they are formed. We owe them this freedom as part of justice. Our lives are greatly affected by what we believe is good and worthy of sacrifice, whether there is a market mechanism or not. The conditions under which we form our beliefs profoundly affect what our preferences turn out to be and what course our lives take.

These interests come apart. Autonomy enables us to freely contribute to our well-being. We have an interest in determining the things that will contribute to our well-being and not only how much well-being we have. These are separate questions and we have an interest in shaping our well-being freely, at stages rejecting or pruning our conceptions of the good, and in advancing those conceptions and accumulating more well-being by better pursuing those things we select.

A further claim is needed to show that the conditions of freedom matter for any plausible theory of distributive justice. This claim is that a just society would allow scope for individuals to act upon their beliefs about the good life at least some of the time. I believe this is a very weak claim indeed. Any reasonable theory of justice will permit individuals to decide for themselves, perhaps within limits, which of the available options to pursue. As such, there is a broad basis for accepting some account of autonomy like the one I described.[18]

Alternative Principles of Sufficient Autonomy

I will now consider a number of rival sufficientarian reasons that appear in the literature and support rival principles of sufficient autonomy. Only one of the thinkers I consider, David Archard, states that his view is a sufficientarian view, but I will argue that while the reasons I derive from their work can help us to illuminate the meaning of sufficient autonomy, they are distinct from, and less plausible than, my approach.

Ronald Dworkin claims that a very weighty, though defeasible, requirement of justice is to secure the circumstances in which citizens' personalities are authentic.[19] Only then, Dworkin claims, can we treat people as equals. We can put this view in other words and state that in order to treat people as equals, we must treat them for who they are and not underdeveloped, stunted or otherwise malformed selves. In this sense, sufficient autonomy is a prerequisite for equal treatment. This requires preparing and maintaining conditions under which we will form authentic personalities. This is a key point since one of the things we are concerned with in autonomy is authenticity. If autonomy is self-rule, then we must identify the authentic self who must rule. Dworkin states that the just society would secure 'Our freedom to engage in activities crucial to forming and reviewing the convictions, commitments, associations, projects, and tastes' because citizens' 'choices should not depend on a view of their personality and of the personalities of others, with whose formation they remain dissatisfied'.[20]

The idea that individuals should not be dissatisfied with their own personalities can be understood as a sufficientarian one, though it may not be understood in this way if we believe that no one can be fully satisfied with their views.[21] The thought of individual contentment as specifying a threshold is familiar from the literature on sufficientarianism.[22] This demand is met once people are satisfied with their own personalities, and until they are satisfied, we should encourage them and provide them with opportunities to obtain such satisfaction. Dworkin's thought seems to be that the familiar bundle of liberal rights of free speech and association will suffice for this purpose but this cannot be so unless these rights are made use of in the correct way. Moreover, we have reason to suspect that subjective satisfaction is not a plausible sufficientarian reason.

This is because dissatisfaction with one's personality cannot ground a proper concern for autonomy. At least it cannot be a sufficient condition for sufficient autonomy. Individual satisfaction is always insufficient unless some degree of autonomy is achieved and this emphasises the importance of sufficient autonomy as part of the conditions of freedom. Consider the following reasons for rejecting dissatisfaction with one's personality as the most plausible sufficientarian reason. One can be wholly satisfied with one's view and be unfree. Indeed, a brainwashed individual may be much more satisfied with his or her choices and personality than someone who has not been brainwashed, for exactly that reason. Such a view of the basis of sufficient autonomy cannot provide a principled defence of the basic liberties of speech and association, with which Dworkin is concerned. We are concerned with the conditions under which we might take a person's satisfaction (or dissatisfaction) with his or her personality seriously. This requires sufficient autonomy to have been already realised. In many ways we are concerned with giving people a certain kind of voice that must be taken seriously and we need some reason or criterion to determine when to do that. Appealing to subjective reports of satisfaction alone cannot do this.

The problem that we face is that satisfying individuals' preferences or ambitions matters sometimes, but it also matters that they have been arrived at in the right way against the right background. This is because there are important ways in which individuals' preferences can be rendered invalid by the conditions in which they live. Indeed, some have thought that it is plausible to believe that individuals' choices make them liable for the costs of such choices, but as I have claimed, this need not be the only reason that we are concerned with the conditions of freedom. An adequate sufficientarian reason to promote autonomy, then, must somehow explain what level of autonomy partly constitutes the social conditions under which people should form and revise their preferences and ambitions. Dworkin's suggestion is instructive and sharpens our focus on what is at stake, but it will not do. We must make at least some of these judgements without recourse to what individuals actually believe about their ambitions and preferences since we are concerned with the conditions under which such beliefs are to be taken seriously.

An alternative sufficientarian reason is suggested by Robert Noggle. Noggle claims that individuals have an interest in becoming full moral agents in addition to simple agents. Simple agents can rationally and intentionally pursue goals, while full moral agents can, in addition, make long-term plans and competently manage their resources.[23] Full moral agents also have, and act upon, a sense of moral decency and have a conception of the good (set of evaluative criteria) that is revisable.[24] Full moral agency is necessary and sufficient for membership in the moral community, in which, Noggle claims, we have a weighty interest. From Noggle's discussion we can articulate a principle of sufficient autonomy. Noggle is concerned with full membership of a community, a key part of which is developing stable preferences for full moral agency. So we might advocate a principle of sufficient autonomy that states that we have a satiable, weighty, non-instrumental, non-egalitarian reason to provide people with sufficient autonomy for stable preferences.

This view faces similar problems to Ronald Dworkin's view. Stable preferences are typically a result of those you are satisfied with. Stable preferences do not really seem to pick out part of the conditions of freedom. Having stable preferences based on misinformation is not to be desired and stability of a preference can be a sign of heteronomy in the face of overwhelming evidence or reason. Because of this, it is clear that we should not rely on Noggle's reason as an adequate sufficientarian reason to promote autonomy. The idea that institutions should be designed so that citizens have stable preferences or are satisfied with their preferences could easily support pursuing policies that limit freedom and curtail autonomy and so it seems implausible to think that this reason could support a plausible principle of sufficient autonomy. This reason is incompatible with our intuitions about the conditions of freedom.

Finally, David Archard argues that we have an interest in holding the correct views about the good life, assurance of which cannot simply come from the fact that we have come to believe that they are the right ones or that they were passed down to us. To make assurance possible one must check their pedigree oneself. People would wish to have this ability to check that their views are true for themselves and to change them if necessary.[25]

Archard claims that we can tailor our conception of autonomy to the degree to which our reasons support the notion, and this must be true. For Archard, then, sufficient autonomy can be specified with reference to the requirement of assurance, which is derived from the interest we have in holding true beliefs. Social institutions should be designed so as to provide citizens with the skills of rational reflection sufficient to assure them that their views about what is worth pursuing are correct or true. However, the idea that assurance of the truth of our preferences is the correct standard is similar to that offered by Noggle and Dworkin. Assurance from checking our beliefs ourselves can be provided by oppressing diversity or by brainwashing, but these are contrary to the conditions of freedom. Moreover, since, for Archard, our interest in assurance is derived from our interest in true beliefs, we can note that brainwashing is compatible with having true beliefs about the good life. Indeed, brainwashing would remove many distractions and possible obstacles to the pursuit of a good life and so, as a bonus, it may be more effective in terms of well-being. However, this view does not quite capture the importance of free adherence and obstructs the conditions of freedom, and so our intuitions rebel against it as a way of specifying a principle of sufficient autonomy as part of the conditions of freedom.

Satisfaction, assurance and stability all seem relevant to individual autonomy, and all seem weighty, satiable, non-egalitarian requirements, but under conditions of freedom one's preferences and ambitions may be unstable for a time, and we may lack assurance of their truth. That we do lack assurance does not cast doubt on whether we form our beliefs under conditions of freedom, as justice demands. Moreover, one may be satisfied and may have stability and assurance, but one may have arrived at this point unreflectively or through being misled. It may plausibly be thought part of the process to entertain doubt and to have a sceptical view for long periods. In the end, everyone, under almost any social conditions and with any level of deliberative power, has settled preferences they are content with.

These three putatively sufficientarian reasons are suggestive and helpful, but they cannot give content to a plausible response to the problem of the conditions of freedom and so we do better to stick with my initial formulation of a principle of sufficient autonomy if we are to defend an indispensable role for sufficient autonomy in distributive justice. What matters is assurance of freedom, not assurance of truth, for the principle of sufficient autonomy.

One can be satisfied with and assured of the truth of one's convictions and one can have stable preferences. However, the fact that we can do so, and are more likely to do so under conditions in which we are not at all free, indicates that such reasons cannot give us a more plausible reason to promote autonomy than the conditions of freedom. Again, we need to know when to take stability of, satisfaction with and assurance of the truth of such beliefs seriously and the sufficientarian reason to live under the conditions of freedom specifies this plausibly. Thus, the aforementioned sufficientarian reasons cannot support an indispensable principle of sufficient autonomy and so do little to support optimism about the prospects for sufficientarianism.

An important sign that a person has secured sufficient autonomy is when he or she can, and is disposed to, give reasons and exchange reasons with others for his or her good. When we have and are willing to discuss critiques of our views, we are free. Only could securing such conditions satisfy and assure the impartial spectator or the party to the original position that one had been choosing freely.[26] Sufficient autonomy, then, constitutes part of the conditions of freedom. Moreover, we should note that the assurance of a spectator in the freedom, not truth, of our beliefs is going to be key to determining sufficient autonomy. As such, a slight alteration to the views considered above could make them plausible.

I have now identified the sufficientarian reason that most plausibly supports a principle of sufficient autonomy as a non-instrumental demand of distributive justice. I have also clarified the meaning of sufficient autonomy by reference to the autonomy required for beliefs about our preferences and ambitions to have been arrived at freely. Sufficient autonomy is the level of deliberative competence that enables us to have assurance from an external point of view that we choose *for ourselves*. This kind of autonomy requires us to be capable of deliberating with others about the reasons that support our conception of the good. We may have weighty reasons to secure more autonomy, but such reasons are distinct from those reasons we have to establish the conditions of freedom, and once we have secured enough there is a shift in the overall profile of reasons we can cite for autonomy-promoting laws and policies.

Alternatives to Sufficient Autonomy

There are alternative ways to try to capture our concern with the conditions of freedom and autonomy that do not refer to a non-instrumental principle of sufficient autonomy. These alternatives can be divided into two types. The first type of alternative denies that sufficient autonomy is required. We could instead distribute autonomy equally, or seek to maximise it. These are non-sufficientarian but non-instrumental principles of autonomy. The second type of alternative accepts the importance of securing sufficient autonomy, but denies that such a principle is non-instrumental. I take these types of view in turn and show that they too are less plausible than the principle of sufficient autonomy, where distinctive.

Equality of Autonomy

One alternative to the principle of sufficient autonomy is the principle of equal autonomy, which requires that we have egalitarian, satiable, non-instrumental, weighty reasons to promote autonomy. Here I understand equality as a satiable demand. I deal with insatiable principles later. One threat to a principle of sufficient autonomy is that if equality is more plausible than sufficiency, then we would not need to appeal to sufficiency, thus there would be no indispensable sufficientarian principle. Later I will provide a general counter-argument to non-satiable principles of autonomy that includes a slightly modified account of equal autonomy.

We could specify equal autonomy in one of two ways and I will argue that both are less plausible than a principle of sufficient autonomy as principles of justice. One version of the principle of equal autonomy would state that justice demands that all people have the same options and the same deliberative powers. However, as I have suggested above, different conceptions of the good may require different levels of deliberative powers and different options for a person to be free. Moreover, some people will wish to enhance their deliberative powers and to enhance or diminish their options as part of their conception of the good and it seems that such variations should be permitted. For example, a judge will require far greater deliberative powers than many others would in order to perform in his or her job well. The inequality here seems unobjectionable. An equality that required levelling down of autonomy would be highly objectionable.

Perhaps to temper this view we would insist on at least a basic minimum level of autonomy. But that basic minimum would be a sufficientarian demand. Moreover, such a view would entail that we must not improve the levels of autonomy of those who want further autonomy, nor diminish the autonomy of those who do want more autonomy, so long as they have enough. It seems, then, that this way of specifying equal autonomy, which rivals the sufficientarian approach, is implausible. Variations in autonomy should be permitted.[27] It seems more plausible to claim that the strength of our reasons to promote autonomy, once we have secured enough, should track our ambitions. Independent of our ambitions, however, we require a certain level of autonomy.[28] This suggests a shift in the reasons we have to promote autonomy and therefore a sufficientarian principle is more plausible than this version of the principle of equal autonomy.

The second way to specify equal autonomy would be to appeal to some idea of equivalence. Where people's options are not the same, they can still be equal because equivalent to one another in some respect. However, equivalence must be calculated with respect to some value to which options and deliberative powers are reducible, for example, expected welfare. On this view, individuals have equal autonomy when their options and deliberative powers are expected to yield, for them, equal welfare scores. Such a principle would not be a fundamental principle of autonomy. This would point towards a more fundamental principle favouring equality of expected welfare. Indeed, to make equivalence judgements we will have to appeal to a dispensable principle of autonomy and so we would not be defending equal autonomy as having fundamental significance; rather, we would be defending equal expected welfare as an indispensable principle. Since individuals' conceptions of the good vary in terms of their complexity, it is unlikely that equal expected welfare, for example, would always require equal autonomy. If equal autonomy is to be worked out in terms of equivalence to equality of some other currency, then there would be no need to refer to equal autonomy, and thus, our reasons applying directly to autonomy could not be weighty, satiable and egalitarian in the sense that rivals the principle of sufficient autonomy. The rival to the principle of sufficient autonomy would be the principle of equal welfare.

Alternatively, we could cash out equivalence in terms of some kind of envy test.[29] If this is how we define equal autonomy, then an equal distribution of autonomy is realised when no one prefers another's level of autonomy. However, prior to making such decisions about whether more autonomy is preferred, choosers would already need some level of autonomy so that our preferences, and our envy, were genuinely our own as the result of a free choice. One can deny this claim only if one insists that autonomy is not a concern of justice. I have already argued that autonomy is a concern of justice. We should be concerned with autonomy if we are concerned with justice since some violations of autonomy are injustices. So the envy test cannot save equivalence as a plausible way of specifying a principle of equal autonomy insofar as it would be a rival to sufficient autonomy. This suggests that our reasons to promote autonomy are non-egalitarian as well as weighty. Now we should ask whether they are, in addition, satiable.

Maximising Autonomy

There are two further principles that deny that there is a non-instrumental shift in our reasons to promote autonomy. In this and the next section I argue against both alternative principles as plausible accounts of how we ought to promote autonomy, and this supports my view that there is a weighty, non-egalitarian and satiable reason to promote autonomy since it is more plausible to hold this view of our reasons than alternatives.

The first rival to sufficient autonomy as a way of articulating our concern with autonomy is an insatiable principle that directs us to maximise autonomy. Ronald Dworkin expresses a view akin to this when he states that authenticity requires the fullest possible opportunity to form and reflect on our convictions, attachments and projects, and opportunity to influence the corresponding opinions of others.[30] The notion of authenticity in Dworkin resembles many of the important aspects of autonomy I sketched earlier including an ability to deliberate about our beliefs.

To avoid compatibility with the principle of sufficient autonomy we must state that the maximisation view is a non-diminishing, insatiable view that recommends that we maximise the sum total of autonomy. As I have articulated the view, sufficientarian principles can be consistent with those views that hold that we always have weighty reasons to promote some good, in our case autonomy, so long as some of those reasons are also non-instrumental and satiable. Both prioritarian and sufficientarian views are indeed consistent with maximisation in that sense. So I discuss the non-diminishing maximisation view as one that states that any single unit of increase in autonomy has the same value and that there is always reason to maximise the aggregate sum of autonomy.

Some infringements of autonomy are clearly more important than others and the non-diminishing maximisation principle cannot account for this. If we assume that the number of options one has can sometimes be used to measure autonomy, then promoting our autonomy in some respects is very important, and not easily outweighed by other considerations, but the same cannot be said for all levels of autonomy. Consider violations of autonomy such as arbitrary arrest, or brainwashing: these are much worse than denying someone one option or denying them access to additional critical thinking education once they are already good critical thinkers. It seems that once we have secured enough, our reasons to promote autonomy, by enhancing reasoning abilities and providing more choices, are far more easily outweighed by other values, like the ability to pursue one particular option further. The level of autonomy we have seems to affect the importance of getting more of it. These intuitions support a non-instrumental shift in our reasons to promote autonomy.

Moreover, such maximisation might see some individuals enjoy a very low level of autonomy, perhaps with very limited deliberative powers as well as few and poor-quality options, while others enjoy great deliberative powers at the expense of other things they would prefer. A common counter-example to maximising principles generally is that they are compatible with some individuals having almost nothing while at the same time many others have very large shares. The plausibility of this objection to principles of maximisation depends on the currency in question, but it seems that all individuals should have at least some level of autonomy. Thus, I conclude that this rival to the sufficientarian approach is implausible because it does not seem that all our weighty, non-egalitarian reasons to promote autonomy are insatiable.

Different Kinds of Violations

Neither a principle of maximisation nor a principle of equality seems to be the correct normative standard for the promotion of autonomy as part of justice. A sufficientarian approach seems to have some structural advantages over rival approaches. Sufficiency has not yet, however, been shown to be required in the most plausible approach to autonomy. It has not been shown that getting sufficient autonomy is especially important in the way that generates a non-instrumental shift in our reasons to promote it. I must now show that a prioritarian principle of autonomy is less plausible than a principle of sufficient autonomy. This prioritarian principle states that we only have weighty, non-egalitarian, insatiable and diminishing reasons to promote individual autonomy.

I have argued in the previous chapter that what distinguishes sufficiency principles from some prioritarian principles is that sufficientarian principles recognise a shift in our reasons to benefit people, whereas determinate prioritarian principles cannot do so without themselves appealing to sufficientarian principles. In order to show that a prioritarian principle must at least appeal to a sufficientarian principle to be plausible, however, it is not enough to show that some violations are worse than others, since uniform prioritarians agree with this. I must show that it is more plausible to claim that once some level of autonomy is achieved, getting more of it is to be determined by different reasons. That is to say, once people have secured sufficient autonomy, further autonomy should be promoted in accordance with a different principle because there is a discontinuity in the rate of change of the marginal weight of our reasons to benefit people further.

A uniform-prioritarian principle of autonomy would claim that those who have the least autonomy should be given priority, and that there is no discontinuity in the rate of change of the marginal weight of our reasons to promote individual autonomy. This would leave no room for sufficientarian principles, but such a prioritarian principle would be incapable of explaining why some violations of autonomy are of a different *kind* than others. If some violations of autonomy are different in kind than others, then this suggests that the most plausible account of the importance of promoting autonomy includes reference to a sufficientarian principle.

First of all, autonomy does not seem to be easily broken down into atomistic units to which we could attach varying degrees of priority. Of course, we can speak intelligibly about one person's being more autonomous than another in that they have more options available or greater deliberative powers, but it is not easy to see how the different components of autonomy can be reduced to one currency amenable to prioritarian understanding. Is one option one unit of autonomy? How are we to understand deliberative powers in unit terms? How many more units of autonomy does a great deliberator have than a poor deliberator? It is not clear that there are answers to these questions, which are important in distinguishing the prioritarian view from the sufficientarian one. Any units we do impose on autonomy will seem arbitrary, not least because our judgements about deliberation are rough and ready and we are not confident about making more fine-grained judgements. Since, when we think we are applying a prioritarian principle, we can only confidently make rough judgements, we may well just be using sufficientarian principles that claim it is important that people have good deliberative powers.[31] If we cannot make fine-grained distinctions all the way up, then it is not clear how the prioritarian principle is required to give us distinctive guidance and therefore it is unclear how the prioritarian principle can be supported by intuitive convictions. Instead, it seems that there are some further advantages to sufficientarian principles in this area.

We are more confident about using categories than making fine-grained judgements, such as 'bad deliberator', 'good deliberator', 'many options', 'few options'.[32] Hard cases fall between these categories but it does not seem like a unit scale would be useful here since we cannot have any confidence in it. Priority could apply to these rough categories, but judgements about how much weight to give to a bad deliberator over a good one would be unclear. Since, in versions of prioritarianism that do not appeal to sufficientarian principles, the extent to which one is badly off is crucial to determine the priority one should receive, and since the principle requires us to make better than rough judgements, the prioritarian principle has serious problems. It seems more likely that there are no fine-grained differences that matter with respect to autonomy.

To support the contention that there is a non-instrumental shift in our reasons, and thus that there is some satiable reason to promote autonomy once people have secured enough, consider the following examples that I believe show that some violations of autonomy, insofar as we are concerned with it for justice, are of a different kind than others.

Imagine Agnes who has been brainwashed though she has many options to choose from. Bernadette has a similar set of options but has the ability to make medium- and long-term plans, can usually spot contradictions in her own judgements and can remedy them. She also makes reasoned assessments of various ways of life and is not being denied information about the costs and benefits of her choices. If we can assist Bernadette or Agnes, we should help Agnes. But the way we work out how to benefit Bernadette is based, to some degree, on whether she wants additional autonomy or not. This is not true for Agnes. It is important for Agnes to be capable of making plans and choosing options whether or not she has the ambition or preference to be more autonomous. Autonomy is important independently of its ability to satisfy her preferences or increase her well-being. The facts that are relevant to determining the importance of benefitting either person seem to change. The case for benefits in each instance is distinct in terms of the reasons they can draw on. This supports some sufficientarian principle.

The Charge of Instrumentality

The second type of alternative to the non-instrumental principle of sufficient autonomy is an instrumental principle. This argumentative strategy accepts a need to accommodate our intuitions about the background conditions of belief formation and concedes that securing sufficient autonomy may have special importance. However, it denies that this importance is best explained by reference to a non-instrumental principle. The instrumental explanation I consider here states that securing sufficient autonomy is an especially important requirement of justice if and only if it has great effects on overall welfare and that welfare should be distributed in accordance with a prioritarian principle. This account of how welfare should be distributed does not need to refer to indispensable sufficientarian principles and so the role of sufficiency is merely coincidental and not indispensable.

I consider arguments from two distinct accounts of how the importance of autonomy is derived from its contribution to welfare, which claim the principle of sufficient autonomy is dispensable because instrumental. I do not consider accounts of how welfare is partly constituted by autonomy and so is derivatively but non-instrumentally significant since those views do not deny that there is a non-instrumental principle of autonomy and as such do not present a final challenge to the indispensability of the principle of sufficient autonomy. I then show that both rivals should be rejected, at least if they are not supplemented by a sufficientarian principle of autonomy, because they provide an implausible account of the conditions of freedom.

A Welfarist Alternative

Some argue that autonomy is valuable only because it is important for welfare, well-being or flourishing, which some say should be distributed in accordance with a prioritarian principle.[33] Such theorists have claimed that autonomy is instrumentally valuable because it usually enhances well-being. If autonomy is only instrumentally valuable, then there is no indispensable role for sufficient autonomy in distributive justice. I shall explain these views and then turn to counter-examples.

In *On Education* Harry Brighouse articulates the view that autonomy is demanded in order to help people live flourishing lives.[34] Providing significant opportunity to flourish is the guiding normative idea for Brighouse. Flourishing lives contain objective goods and are endorsed from within.[35] This means that to contribute to our flourishing the way of life we pursue must be good for reasons independent of our choosing that life and we must accept that this way of life is good for us. This view holds that justice demands education for the skills of autonomy, and rational and critical reflection, because they are reliable guides to discovering good ways of life we can endorse from within and this forms an essential part of the conditions under which everyone has significant opportunity to flourish.[36]

This view is a rival to the principle of sufficient autonomy if it claims also that autonomy is only valuable in this way. Brighouse eschews attaching non-instrumental importance to autonomy in order to avoid making the controversial claim that many proponents of clearly good ways of life could not accept.[37] His argument is given wider scope by appealing to autonomy as having an important, though instrumental, role in an account of well-being which he believes can be widely endorsed. Therefore, it seems apt to consider this view a rival to and incompatible with the principle of sufficient autonomy since Brighouse accepts that we have reason to avoid appealing to premises that endorse the non-instrumental importance of autonomy.

The requirement of endorsement from within, on the view discussed by Brighouse, is similar to the satisfaction condition employed by Ronald Dworkin. The way of life we pursue must be one we believe is good for us. According to this view, we must have the opportunity to enter a number of ways of life because we may not be able to live some good ways of life from within. Insofar as autonomy improves the chances of securing significant opportunity to flourish for all, it is valuable and should be promoted.

As a response to the conditions of freedom this view recommends that individuals should form their beliefs under conditions in which they have significant opportunity to flourish. If such conditions include the general rights and liberties that are associated with that freedom, then, we may think that there is no need for a special non-instrumental justification of autonomy to account for our intuitions. A commitment of this view is that the conditions of freedom require the deliberative powers of autonomy, but if and when these powers do not contribute to securing significant opportunity to flourish, they are not important, and when they detract from opportunity to flourish, they are to be avoided. Thus, the defender of this view can claim that if sufficient autonomy is especially important, it is especially important wholly because of the contribution it makes to preserving significant opportunity to flourish for all. Here the shift in our reasons to promote autonomy takes place at the instrumental level and so, if this view is sound, this shift cannot support an indispensable sufficientarian principle that applies to autonomy. At best it can support an instrumental principle of sufficient autonomy quite different in content from the one I have proposed.

A second welfarist view I consider is expounded by Richard Arneson.[38] Arneson suggests that prioritising the worse off in respect of well-being can explain the wrongness of stunting individuals' ambitions. A commitment of this view is that manipulating our ambitions is permissible or even demanded by justice, if it works to the long-term benefit of the least advantaged. This does seem to pick out what is wrong with many of the norms we find objectionable. One of the reasons we object to women's ambitions being affected by social norms about what counts as feminine conduct is because women are generally made worse off by them.[39] These arguments suggest that the conditions of freedom are not non-instrumentally important but rather, are only important because they are a means to prioritising the welfare of the worse off in the long term. Sufficient autonomy for all is required only when it is to the advantage of the least advantaged and this, it seems, will not always provide us with sufficient autonomy that seemed sound from the section on autonomy. This objection to sufficient autonomy can be supported if our intuitions about the conditions of freedom can be explained by this instrumental principle. Thus, both of these views pose the same threat to the view I have defended, namely that a non-instrumental principle of justice applying to autonomy is less plausible than its rivals and so is not indispensable.

Some Counter-examples

I now consider counter-examples to the aforementioned rivals to the principle of sufficient autonomy. I take the following counter-examples to show that those views are highly implausible and since the principle of sufficient autonomy successfully negotiates them, these are decisive considerations in favour of the indispensability of the principle of sufficient autonomy.

Imagine that there is a pill such that, should someone take it and they conceive children, their children will come to be capable of identifying with any view about the good life that contains objective goods, as the first account of the instrumental role of autonomy demands. The pill will mould the unborn child's character and composition so that he or she can live that way of life from the inside, as Brighouse's view of flourishing requires. On this view, if such a pill were available, then we ought to use it, if it is the most effective way to provide significant opportunity to flourish, which it seems it would be. Moreover, we could design society so that it facilitated some particular good way of life and it was the same for everyone. This way we do not need to provide individuals with the powers of critical reflection and deliberation because they can already flourish as things are and so have significant opportunity to flourish. In such cases we may not even require basic liberties. If this pill were available, then there would be no need to make individuals autonomous, to have deliberative powers or deliberative inclinations, even though in our current society it may be a reliable way to provide all with significant opportunity to flourish.

This example shows that those who believe that the value of autonomy can be wholly reduced to its instrumental value cannot provide us with a full account of the importance of autonomy. It is plausible to claim that autonomy possesses some instrumental value but we must allow room for a non-instrumental concern with autonomy that the principle of sufficient autonomy captures. Surely justice demands that we forgo the pill and allow people to grow up under conditions of freedom, making their own mistakes, perhaps, and finding their own way? Predetermining our convictions about the good life and by-passing the deliberative procedures associated with autonomy is clearly unjust. Even if we do have reason to prescribe the pill, it would still be important for individuals to deliberate for reasons of freedom. On the rival view, we would have no reason to prescribe sufficient autonomy.

This counter-example, we may think, does not help us to judge Arneson's view, which holds that we should give priority to the worse off in respect of welfare when designing social institutions. It is clear that for Arneson whether to take the pill is a somewhat open question since it might not respect the priority we should give to the worse off. Of course, if one can identify with any life, then the welfare costs of regret or of pursuing the wrong course are avoided and so, other things being equal, it will be better for all. However, other things may not be equal and so to provide a more convincing response to Arneson's view we must advance a further counter-example.

A society that inculcates the cheapest tastes in its child-members through advertising, education and a general ethos will be able to more effectively advance the well-being of its members. Ensuring citizens' ambitions and preferences are cheaper to fulfil will enable society to advance the well-being scores of more people, and to a greater extent, with the same resources than if everyone had expensive tastes. This society would be more just according to the prioritarian welfarist principle. This course of action, however, seems clearly unjust. If individuals' choices, beliefs and actions are essentially determined by their social conditions, which more

75

or less coerce them into having, without deliberation, only the cheapest ambitions, then that society cannot be just.

What is wrong in the pill and the cheap tastes cases is that they are compatible with a failure of freedom and failure to use our latent capacity for deliberation. The principle of sufficient autonomy leaves room for other things to matter, unlike upper limit sufficientarianism, and perhaps once people have secured sufficient autonomy, we should promote the welfare of the least advantaged, at the cost of further options and deliberative abilities for others. Perhaps the only further justification for more options and deliberative abilities is that they improve the welfare of the worse off, but sufficient autonomy has special significance and is not reducible to a concern with prioritising the worse off in terms of their welfare.

The Principle of Sufficient Autonomy and Counter-examples

I shall now show that the principle of sufficient autonomy helps us to negotiate these counter-examples far better than the welfarist principles, and is more plausible and therefore indispensable.

In the case of the pill, individuals have their life plans determined much like those in Huxley's *Brave New World*. In a less extreme way we can say that family circumstances or genetics determine or predispose us to certain ways of life, and may be, to a lesser degree, objectionable. The principle of sufficient autonomy insists that, if it is possible to genetically predispose a child to a certain way of life, or if families encourage some particular conception of the good, the child and the adult he or she becomes can give reasons for why they believe as they do, and will willingly exchange reasons with others in a deliberative process.[40] Only when such background conditions of society as a whole are preserved do they have reason to be assured that they are not manipulated, and that their choice is free.

In the case of cheap tastes, individuals are denied the opportunity to reflect upon what is of value, whether cheap or otherwise, and to be challenged by others. They are denied the opportunity to use their deliberative powers and to act upon the verdicts they reach to give content to their own well-being. In such cases autonomy is still important. The principle of sufficient autonomy requires preferences and beliefs to be formed in a deliberative environment. This requires that all have a disposition to reason with others about the costs that are reasonable or unreasonable to impose on others. Thus, these counter-examples show the relative plausibility of the non-instrumental element of the principle of sufficient autonomy and help support its indispensability in a complete and sound account of distributive justice.

Conclusion

My aim in this chapter was to show that the principle of sufficient autonomy is both distinctive and more plausible than rival principles, and is therefore indispensable to a complete and sound theory of distributive justice. I began by sketching autonomy and showing that it is both important for justice and something we can have more or less of. This raises the question of whether it should be distributed in accordance with a sufficientarian or other distributive principle. I then surveyed some sufficientarian reasons that may support a sufficientarian principle for autonomy and explained how these reasons may help us respond to the problem of the conditions of freedom required for belief formation. The final stage of the argument demonstrated the superiority of this account, which makes essential reference to a shift in our reasons to benefit people once they have enough, to alternative ways of understanding the importance of autonomy. The first alternatives were non-sufficientarian principles, such as the principle of equal autonomy. The second alternative was a welfare view, which sought to explain autonomy in instrumental terms. Having taken these steps I have shown that the principle of sufficient autonomy is more plausible than its rival instrumental or non-sufficientarian alternatives. I have also vindicated the sufficientarian reasons line of argument, which may be used to identify and defend other sufficientarian principles.

In the next chapter I shall consider the extent of the role that this principle should have in our thought as this also affects the prospects for sufficientarianism. In particular, I will look at the extent of the role this principle should have in debates about educational justice and show that the principle should have an extensive role indeed.

Notes

1. Christman and Anderson, *Autonomy and the Challenges to Liberalism*, 3.
2. Christman, 'Constructing the inner citadel'.
3. In Rawls, *Justice as Fairness*, 45, the author states that 'A second way of drawing up a list of basic rights and liberties is analytical: we consider what liberties provide the political and social conditions essential for the adequate development and full exercise of the two moral powers of free and equal persons.' In Raz, *The Morality of Freedom*, 406, the author states that 'The moral virtues associated with the diverse forms of life allowed by a morality which enables all normal persons to attain autonomy by moral means are very likely to depend on character traits many of which lead to intolerance of other acceptable forms of life. All those forms of life are not only legitimate but morally required if all persons are to have autonomy. Therefore respect for autonomy by requiring competitive value-pluralism also establishes the necessity of toleration.'
4. In Rawls, *Justice as Fairness*, 131, the author states that 'The case for the two principles can be strengthened by spelling out in more detail the notion of a free person. Very roughly the parties regard themselves as having a highest-order interest in how all their other interests, including even their fundamental ones, are shaped and regulated by social institutions.' At ibid., 475, the author states: 'Thus the persons in the original position are moved by a certain hierarchy of interests. They must first secure their highest-order interest and fundamental aims (only the general form of which is known to them), and this fact is reflected in the precedence they give to liberty; the acquisition of means that enable them to advance their other desires and ends has a subordinate place.'
5. Raz, *The Morality of Freedom*, 372–8.
6. In Dworkin, *Sovereign Virtue*, 159–60, the author states that 'any auction scheme approved by equality of resources requires, for example, some baseline principle specially protecting the parties'

freedom to engage in activities crucial to forming and reviewing the convictions, commitments, associations, projects, and tastes that they bring to the auction and, after the auction, to the various decisions about production and trade that will reform and redistribute their initial holdings'.

7. In Dworkin, *The Theory and Practice of Autonomy*, 80, the author states that 'what does have intrinsic value is not having choices but being recognised as the kind of creature who is capable of making choices. That capacity grounds our idea of what it is to be a person and moral agent equally worthy of respect by all.'

8. Sen, 'Equality of what?'

9. In Rawls, *A Theory of Justice*, 131–2, the author states that 'free persons conceive of themselves as beings who can revise and alter their final ends and who give first priority to preserving their liberty in these matters. Hence, they not only have final ends that they are in principle free to pursue or reject, but their original allegiance and continued devotion to these ends are to be formed and affirmed under conditions that are free.'

10. Rawls, *Justice as Fairness*, 18–19.

11. Ibid., 18–19.

12. Mason, 'Equality, social responsibility and gender socialisation'.

13. Rawls, *Political Liberalism*, 332.

14. Rawls, *Justice as Fairness*, 24.

15. Ibid., 222.

16. In Fleurbaey, *Fairness, Responsibility, and Welfare*, 269, the author states that 'For individuals above the threshold, the concern for freedom is captured in this approach in two ways. First, the dimension of choice can be taken as one dimension of quality of life among others . . . Second, the approach respects individual preferences and therefore seeks to provide individuals with the combination of life dimensions that they desire. On the other hand, this approach does not fetishise choice and opportunities, and puts the satisfaction of preferences above the provision of opportunities, except when the basic level of freedom and autonomy is at stake.'

17. Dworkin, *Sovereign Virtue*, 65–119.

18. I do not assume that all violations/infringements of the conditions of freedom are infringements or violations of autonomy, but rather that the cases I discussed in the section on autonomy establish that the conditions in which beliefs are formed can manifest injustice.

19. Dworkin, *Sovereign Virtue*, 158–61.

20. Ibid., 159.

21. I considered this interpretation of Dworkin's view when discussing maximising autonomy in the section on autonomy.
22. The idea that satisfaction is a sufficientarian criterion is first introduced in Frankfurt, 'Equality as a moral ideal', and is used in Huseby, 'Sufficiency'.
23. Noggle, 'Special agents'.
24. Ibid., 110–14.
25. In Archard, 'Children, multiculturalism, and education', 146, the author states: 'Her assurance that her values are correct cannot come simply from the fact that these values were passed onto her by her parents. She must also be assured that those values by which she believes have the right pedigree. Arguably this requires that she has been able critically and rationally to examine these values and has not found them wanting. This will not guarantee that her values are the right ones. But in the absence of any such autonomous scrutiny she can have no assurance that they are. The upshot is that she would not want merely to inherit a set of values from her parents. She would wish also to be equipped with the ability for her own part to review, and to confirm or to repudiate her inherited ideals.'
26. Rawls, *A Theory of Justice*, 15–19; Smith et. al., *The Theory of the Moral Sentiments*, 110.
27. Marc Fleurbaey uses the term 'equality of autonomy' to describe his own view, but it much more closely resembles a sufficientarian view of autonomy. For details, see Fleurbaey, *Fairness, Responsibility, and Welfare*, 272.
28. Dworkin, *Sovereign Virtue*.
29. Ibid., 67–8.
30. In ibid., 160, the author states that 'Authenticity has both a passive and an active voice: participants to the auction would want both an opportunity to form and reflect on their own convictions, attachments, and projects, and an opportunity to influence the corresponding opinions of others, on which their own success in the auction in large part depends ... Ideal authenticity requires the fullest possible opportunity not because people are always more likely to make wise choices with more time but because their choices should not depend on a view of their personality and of the personalities of others, with whose formation they remain dissatisfied.'
31. The point I am making against prioritarian principles echoes Rawls's remarks about the difference principle justifying a social minimum. For details, see Rawls, *A Theory of Justice*, 278.

32. Such distinctions would need to be possible to establish a sufficiency threshold.
33. Arneson and Shapiro, 'Democratic autonomy and religious liberty'; Arneson, 'Against Rawlsian equality of opportunity'; Arneson, 'Welfare should be the currency of justice'; Brighouse, *On Education*; Raz, *The Morality of Freedom*.
34. In Brighouse, *On Education*, 15, the author states that 'the argument that education should facilitate autonomy depends on the idea that autonomy plays an important role in enabling people to live flourishing lives'.
35. In ibid., 15–16, the author states that 'Flourishing lives have two things in common. First, for a life to be truly worthwhile it must contain objective goods . . . but having objectively good things in one's life is not enough for a flourishing life. For somebody actually to flourish, they have to identify with the life they are leading.'
36. In ibid., 18–19, the author states that 'providing the opportunity to enter ways of life requires that the state educate children in the skills of rational reflection and comparison usually associated with autonomy . . . [for] the basic methods for rational evaluation are reliable aids to uncovering how to live well, and they are the only such aids that can be identified and taught'.
37. Ibid., 15.
38. Arneson, 'Welfare should be the currency of justice'.
39. Fleurbaey, *Fairness, Responsibility, and Welfare*; Mason, 'Equality, personal responsibility and gender socialisation'.
40. For a view of autonomy that also supports condemning parents' choices to genetically predispose a child to some conception of the good, see Clayton, *Justice and Legitimacy in Upbringing*, 102–6.

4   Sufficiency and Education

As I argued in Chapter 1, the prospects for sufficientarianism do not only depend upon there being an indispensable sufficientarian principle(s). They also depend on the extent of the role those principles should play in our thought about practical debates. Having established that the principle of sufficient autonomy is indispensable, it must play some role in our thought. The extent of the role a principle plays in our thought depends upon a number of factors including whether and how it fits with other plausible demands of justice and whether it can help to resolve some problems in ongoing debates.

If the principle of sufficient autonomy has little to say in terms of policy implications, could not shed light on the various problems in those debates and did not fit alongside, or was always outweighed by, accepted and plausible demands in that area, then the principle could not have an extensive role in our thought. Though it has some role in our thought, such a principle would do less to improve the prospects for sufficientarianism than a principle that had important implications for policy, resolved some problems in various debates and could fit in well alongside some of the plausible demands of justice in the relevant areas.

In this chapter, I explain four contributions that the principle of sufficient autonomy makes to debates about education. Taken together, these contributions give strong support to the claim that the prospects for sufficientarianism are good.

I begin by discussing the relationship between education, justice and autonomy. I show that education is an important site for justice and injustice and that the principle of sufficient autonomy makes demands of the design of educational institutions.

82

Subsequent sections show that these demands are plausible and fit well or help resolve problems with existing views. Some of these advantages are due to the particular contents of the principle of sufficient autonomy, but others are due primarily to the shift aspect of sufficientarianism.

I then show that the principle of sufficient autonomy can help us in justifying education for autonomy to groups who may reject it, such as the Old Order Amish. In particular, the shift in the importance of autonomy, which is unique to sufficientarian principles, offers a more helpful way of reframing this debate. I argue that the principle of sufficient autonomy, understood as partly constituting the intrinsically valuable conditions of freedom, provides us with a more decisive argument than instrumental arguments for autonomy and helps us to delineate the kinds of education that cannot be easily opted out of, and the kinds of education that can more easily be outweighed by countervailing considerations.

I then draw out a key demand of sufficient autonomy: the requirement of an education to facilitate the discovery and development of talents and interests for autonomy. This requirement makes two further important contributions to debates about educational justice. First, in helping to clarify Rawls's principle of fair equality of opportunity by resolving an ambiguity in the meaning of 'talent' and supplementing this principle with a baseline of talent development. Second, in helping to defend that principle against some powerful criticisms that have been made of it by Richard Arneson.

In the final argumentative section of this chapter I show that the role for sufficiency in debates about justice and education is more plausible than previous sufficientarian approaches to education. I will argue that the principle of sufficient autonomy is more plausible than the accounts of educational adequacy offered by Elizabeth Anderson and Debra Satz because those accounts are vulnerable to the old objections to sufficientarianism, whereas the principle of sufficient autonomy is not, by virtue of its shift. These contributions show that the principle of sufficient autonomy should have an extensive role in our thought and this supports optimism about the prospects for sufficientarianism.

Before going any further it is worth restating the principle of sufficient autonomy and the conditions of its being satisfied, which were originally formulated in the last chapter:

> *The Principle of Sufficient Autonomy*: We have weighty, non-instrumental, satiable reasons to provide people with autonomy sufficient for the conditions of freedom.

In the previous chapter I articulated what this meant in more detail. Autonomy sufficient for the conditions of freedom is achieved (1) when individuals are capable of articulating and defending their own views, (2) have a disposition to exchange reasons with others, and (3) are well positioned with regards to relevant information so as to establish third-person assurance of the freedom, not truth, of their beliefs.

Autonomy, Education and Justice

Education is a process through which an individual learns, acquires and develops knowledge, skills and competencies. Our educational experiences have a defining impact on our lives. Our performance whilst attending educational institutions affects our chances of securing certain jobs and benefits, and our experience of education influences what we can and want to do in our leisure time. Education has a significant impact on how we are able to contribute to our well-being and our ability to control our lives. Because education deeply affects the lives of individuals, we should be concerned with the kind of education provided and how it is distributed between individuals.

Moreover, evaluations of how well a government or society is performing are often cashed out in terms of educational statistics. Evaluations of development and success internationally tend to cite literacy rates as one key measure. When we reflect upon the value of our own educational experiences, whether with regret or other feelings, we find that there are a number of ways in which education can and does contribute to the value of our lives. While our school days may or may not be 'the best days of our lives', as people often say, they are certainly some of the most important.

Because of the influence of educational provision on our lives, judgements about such provision will form part of our overall assessment of the justice of society. Citizens have some important interests in the goods education makes available and, in a just society, provision of education will be arranged in a way that respects these interests. The state cannot refuse to get involved with education and simply allow private individuals to provide for it. To do so would be to allow educational provision to be distributed in a particular way that may fail to recognise citizens' rightful claims. If educational systems were designed so that many citizens received so little opportunity that they could not contribute to their own well-being and were denied opportunities to discover and pursue their own fulfilment, then that society would be unjust. Thus, education is importantly linked to sound assessments of justice.

Often it is not easy to tell if a piece of legislation or a particular change in curriculum makes society more just. We could assess these changes, which affect education, in an ad hoc way, making reference to whatever our strongest convictions are at the time. However, those judgements are likely to conflict and be insensitive to many of the important values at stake that are not immediately obvious. This kind of myopia is the hallmark of bad policy, and incoherence and inconsistency can render our actions self-defeating. Moreover, we often find ourselves pulled in different directions by different ad hoc considerations and the only way to resolve these conflicts is to appeal to some principle that survives reflection.

This leads us to look to general principles to help resolve these problems. In order to make judgements that we can have confidence in, we must make reference to an appropriate normative standard that has been derived by critically scrutinising our strongest convictions in this area and organising them into a respectable whole in the form of a rule, principle or theory.

Education can affect our autonomy by affecting our ability and willingness to choose for ourselves and to act in accordance with that choice. A principle of justice applying to autonomy will have implications for educational institutions that tend to play a major role in our development from child to adult. We can see that the principle of sufficient autonomy bears on education by noting that commonly given reasons for valuing education are themselves related to autonomy. This will justify the attention I give to the educational context as an important one for the implications of the principle of sufficient autonomy, though it may also have important implications for other areas.

To work out why something is valuable and under what conditions, it is sensible to begin with the most commonly given reasons for valuing it. A commonly given reason for valuing education is that it will enhance job prospects. Enhanced job prospects means an improvement in the job options available to an individual. Improvements can occur along different dimensions. For example, education can be the difference between having a job available to you and not. An education can also make available jobs with more flexible working hours, a greater likelihood of promotion and greater job security. All of these factors enhance the job prospects of an individual and can be achieved through education.

The next step is to ask if enhanced job prospects are valuable only because greater remuneration and other benefits are usually attached. If they are, then enhanced job prospects are not always valuable but are instead valuable only because attached to these other benefits. In our description of the value of education we could, then, leave out all reference to enhanced prospects and instead refer to the conditions that give enhanced job prospects value. When deciding how education should be distributed, we must bear in mind the conditions under which, and the reasons why, it is valuable. This will give us a clearer and more accurate account of the value of education. However, in this case we cannot ask if enhanced job prospects would be valuable even if they did not improve your set of job options along the dimensions discussed above. This is because these improvements just are what it means to have enhanced job prospects. If, as a result of a better education, you had other job options open to you but they did not represent an improvement in your position, your job prospects would not have been enhanced. We must, then, take each aspect of enhanced job prospects and ask whether it is valuable in itself and if not, what for, and so on and so forth until we have an account of what is fundamentally valuable.

When thinking about what improves one's job prospects, we should begin by assessing why one might value increased remuneration. To do this we ask: if additional education only increases the expected remuneration of one's prospective jobs, how does one benefit, and does one always benefit? Income is important for a variety of reasons but it is certainly not intrinsically valuable. An increase in income is only important because it makes other goods available to us. These are goods that are essential for our survival and good functioning such as clothing, shelter, and food and drink. Income also helps us acquire goods that help satisfy our preferences and make our lives easier, like fast cars, Everton FC season tickets and Roxy Music albums. These items contribute to the well-being of at least some people, though some items will have a greater significance than others. So, insofar as education affects our job prospects along the dimension of remuneration and income, we have a reason to value education.

The value of increased income is dependent on the interests of the recipient of the income. Whether extra remuneration is valuable depends on your aims (both given and chosen) and your capacity to fulfil them, for example, by money's ability to meet the cost of certain goods. It is certainly not valuable to have extra wealth and income if it cannot help you acquire things that you value or need to flourish. However, it is possible that you could have too much income and for your life to become less fulfilling as a result, just as too many options may lead to worse choices. Extra remuneration, it seems, only enhances your job prospects if it helps you to fulfil certain aims. Improvements in your working hours, working conditions and the flexibility of this work are valuable too because they can contribute to the fulfilment of these aims.

Another way that one's job prospects may be enhanced by education is if education makes available additional valuable job opportunities. I believe there are two ways this may happen. First, a job may provide you with the opportunity to exercise your talents to a greater extent and/or give you an opportunity to develop new talents. One may want to take on a promotion or do a different job in order to develop or make use of developed talents in ways that one would not have been able to otherwise.

One sometimes has a reason to choose a job that is better in this respect but the same in all other respects such as job security, flexible working hours and remuneration. Second, job prospects may be enhanced by additional opportunities if a job becomes available that can help you to directly fulfil an ambition central to your conception of the good. Some may realise the value of working for the public good in areas such as politics, law, education and health. Some may realise ambitions by gardening or by seeing that what they do does some good for others or for the natural world. Education contributes to the quality of our lives by making available jobs that give us access to these goods, but it can also contribute to the realisation of intrinsic goods in our leisure time. For example, one might be able to realise the goods associated with gardening, cooking and building, all of which require the development of certain skills and accompanying knowledge, and all of which can contribute to an individual's flourishing. This too can ground a claim for education and gives us a reason to provide it in a certain fashion. So, education is valuable for the part it plays in making jobs available that help us to fulfil our goals. This is achieved by making available goods like exercise of our talents or by making available means to fulfil and pursue our chosen and given aims in our leisure time through remuneration and better working conditions. But how are these linked to autonomy?

Although it is true that all human beings are born with some important interests, these are not exhaustive of our interests over a complete life. If human life was merely structured around our basic needs, our lives would consist solely of feeding ourselves and keeping out of harm and this is not the kind of life anyone really aspires to, even if this is the reality for many in our world. In forming our ambitions we need to have a reasoning ability more expansive than the one required for our given aims of sustaining our life through eating, drinking, and staying warm and safe. This is because it is important that we are able to make decisions about what constitutes the good life and what means are available to achieve them. We also need to be able to decide whether these ends are truly important and whether the means we have at our disposal could not be improved by being altered in some way. The development of our own talents is one way in which we alter the means at our disposal because when we cultivate skills, we change the ways in which we can achieve our ends and the kinds of ends available to us. We require a reasoning ability so that we can develop, revise and pursue our important interests. Without this reasoning ability our lives are bound to be undirected. As we saw in the previous chapter, directing ourselves towards goals freely is an important part of autonomy and justice, and now we see that it is linked to the value of education and the principle of sufficient autonomy. This is the role I have in mind for the principle of sufficient autonomy in education.

This intuitive examination of the value of education for the possessor has clarified some of the values and interests at stake when distributing education. The value of education is linked to our well-being and also to the reasoning and deliberative abilities needed to develop, revise and pursue our way of life, as well as the abilities to develop and use our talents. This shows that education is concerned with autonomy and a principle of autonomy will have implications for educational provision. However, the principle does not exhaust the demands of justice in education.

Education for Autonomy

One specific debate regarding the value of autonomy relative to other important values has implications for educational provision in the just society. The legal case that usually frames this debate is *Wisconsin v. Yoder*.[1] The general details of this particular case will suffice to explain the general problem that the principle of sufficient autonomy can help us to solve.

Some parents and members of traditional religious communities do not want their child-members to receive certain kinds of education. Members of these communities do not want their child-members to receive education about certain forms of behaviour or belief that the community holds to be wrongful, sinful or otherwise corrupting, disorientating or distracting from the pursuit of their particular form of the good life. In particular, communities have opposed certain forms of sex education, as well as competitive sports and some academic subjects. They have opposed such education on the grounds that it frustrates the ability of their children to live a good life.[2]

Whether we should insist on educating these children for autonomy, against their parents' wishes, depends on the weight of the conflicting demands in each case, which include autonomy and other concerns such as religious freedom, parental partiality and the child's well-being.[3] If a sufficientarian principle is the correct approach to understanding the demands of autonomy, as I have argued, then the case for some form of education for autonomy will be more important than others and so we should be able to shed light on the issue of when and why parents can withdraw children from compulsory education and under what conditions it is more easily justified. If parents have good reasons, either of well-being or parental partiality, then they will have more traction against supra-threshold education for autonomy than sub-threshold education for autonomy.

The principle of sufficient autonomy provides us with a principled basis for arguing for some level of autonomy that is much less easily outweighed by countervailing considerations. This makes the debate about parental removal of children from public education more tractable than it has seemed. A sufficientarian account of the value of autonomy helps us to see more clearly what kind of autonomy we have most reason to provide and that part of autonomy that may be more easily outweighed by legitimate concerns of traditional communities like the Amish. This is achieved by the shift, which separates the weightiest demands for improvements in autonomy from less weighty demands for improvements. It is not in virtue of the particular content of the principle. In addition, the sufficientarian claim highlights that level of autonomy that it is most important to achieve. I will argue that the principle of sufficient autonomy, then, plays a quite extensive role in our thought about this important practical debate and has key advantages over instrumental accounts of the value of autonomy in this regard. In order to show this, I will now set out the alternative solutions to the disagreement.

The Solution

Having shared interests with one's family and community can make an important contribution to well-being.[4] Also, it seems that parents should have some decision-making ability with respect to their children. This may well extend to the type of education they receive, including what type of school they attend and what sorts of classes they take. The freedom afforded to parents to live religious lives in traditional communities, like the Amish, seems to commit us to allowing them to bring up their children in that way. Thus, there is both a theoretical and a practical question. The theoretical question is: accepting that parents should have some control over what their children do, what kinds of education can children be exempted from? The practical question is: given that parents do in fact have a lot of control over what happens to their children, how can we frame a practical debate about exempting children from a certain sort of education? The principle of sufficient autonomy can shed some light on the answers to these normative questions in ways that are more plausible than alternatives.

There are two main differences between the arguments that can be given by a sufficientarian in response to the claims of traditional communities and the arguments that are given by one prominent liberal view. Both of these differences, I will argue, make the sufficientarian approach relatively more helpful. These features are, first, that the sufficientarian argument attaches non-instrumental importance to autonomy while other arguments do not. The liberal arguments I consider to be rivals only argue for autonomy on the basis of its instrumental role in promoting well-being and this leads to important problems when considering questions about when parents can remove their children from certain types of education because the argument does not come down decisively either way. The second difference between the sufficientarian approach and these rivals is that the sufficientarian approach differentiates between aspects of autonomy as being more important but not linked to well-being and so helps to delineate areas of easier compromise, which is much needed in the practical debates about this issue. The argument for sufficient autonomy highlights the kinds of education for autonomy for which an exemption should never or not easily be granted. This provides us with a focal point or pivot for a practical but nevertheless normatively attractive compromise.

The Value of a Non-instrumental Argument

Many arguments for autonomy-supporting education point to its instrumental value. In the previous chapter I considered Brighouse's instrumental argument for autonomy. Brighouse argues that the powers of autonomy are a reliable guide to identifying a number of good ways of life. Thus, autonomy has an important role in realising significant opportunity to flourish. I have not argued that autonomy has no such instrumental value. I have merely argued that it is less plausible to think that autonomy's value is wholly instrumental than to think that autonomy has some non-instrumental value. In this section, I will argue that it is less helpful, and not only less plausible, to think that autonomy only has non-instrumental value when addressing this particular debate about education.

Instrumental arguments for autonomy claim that educating for the skills of autonomy is important because autonomy promotes our well-being. Being autonomous with respect to our conceptions of the good life helps us to serve our well-being better than if we had been directed by others. If autonomy has a tendency to improve our lives, then we have reason to promote autonomy and to educate for autonomy. This is what some have called the core defensible part of autonomy.[5]

It is plausible to think that education for autonomy has significant well-being benefits in helping us to spot contradictions in our own views and in helping us to understand alternative ways of life but the instrumental argument used to support education for autonomy can be used to support the exemption for education for autonomy too. This can be seen without making the controversial claim that only autonomous lives can be flourishing lives. However, it should be observed that traditional or religious communities, who would like to remove their children from some or all public educational institutions, could utilise the instrumental argument to support their conclusion along the following lines. Children should be removed from educational institutions when it threatens their ability to live a good life. A good deal of what is learnt at schools will turn out to be useless for children. This is especially so in the case of *Wisconsin v. Yoder*, because the disputed education essentially educates them to pass exams to qualify them for jobs they will never have. It would be far better for those children to work within their community and develop, to a higher degree, their own talents and skills which can be used to directly improve their well-being and the well-being of their traditional community.

Instrumental arguments can support either conclusion. It might be the case that we promote a person's well-being by insisting they attend certain classes that their parents do not want them to attend, but it might also be the case that they are better off not attending. This disagreement can only be resolved by establishing which course of action will have the greatest instrumental benefits and this is not clear either way. Which option will yield the greatest well-being turns on our conception of well-being, but this, quite obviously, is the main bone of contention here. Those in traditional communities will claim that well-being consists in a certain way of life that requires removal from schooling, and those who posit the instrumental argument will claim that their well-being is best served by being educated for autonomy. There may be reasonable disagreement about the good life, and there is certainly a deep practical disagreement which cannot be overcome merely by stating that those who disagree are wrong, but first I want to discuss the theoretical problem.

The theoretical problem is that an instrumental argument cannot clearly win the day. It simply pushes the issue back to questions about the nature of well-being. However, insofar as these instrumental arguments seem to tell in favour of one choice, they seem to tell in favour of the Amish parents. If autonomy is justified in virtue of the instrumental benefits it confers on its possessor, then the correct policy would be to have some kind of exemption for those in traditional communities, assuming that it is possible to flourish in such ways of life, which should be a starting assumption of any moderately charitable engagement with their argument. Some traditional communities do allow their children to opt out as they come of age. If the concern is with well-being, and autonomy is not necessary for it, and if traditional communities do offer a good way of life, then there is little reason to think a blanket policy of education for autonomy is justified by an instrumental concern for well-being.

If we can single out autonomy as having special significance, significance beyond a contribution to well-being, then we may be able to succeed in finding an argument that can justify children being educated for autonomy, at least theoretically. There is such an argument, and it is an argument from the importance of the conditions of freedom to the principle of sufficient autonomy. If such an argument is sound, and I have argued that it is in the previous chapter, then we can by-pass discussion of the instrumental importance of education for autonomy and instead say that freedom requires education for autonomy. It is no longer a matter of weighing up the instrumental benefits of compulsory education, and the instrumental benefits of avoiding it for particular groups.

Of course, members of certain traditional communities will not accept this. They will claim that their children should not be free if being free means eternal damnation, for example. This is a deep and lasting disagreement on an important normative issue. However, we will be able to provide non-instrumental grounds that more decisively support the conclusion that we should educate for autonomy. The instrumental argument could support either conclusion and it seems plausible to think that it will support the conclusion that children from traditional communities can opt out in many cases.

A Sufficientarian Approach

As I have rehearsed the disagreement above we see two conflicting points of view. There are, on the one hand, those who believe that education for autonomy is instrumentally valuable and, on the other hand, those who believe that it is not and favour an option to withdraw their children from it on grounds of well-being. I believe that the distinctive feature of sufficientarianism – the shift

– helps us to deal with a problem of justice in a way that renders it amenable to a compromise in practice.

Recall that the distinctive feature of sufficientarianism is that it claims that there is a shift, or discontinuity in the rate of change of the marginal weight of our reasons to benefit people further once they have secured enough. This technicality can seem obscure, so it is worth bearing in mind the more intuitive explanation. The basic idea of the shift is that we have weighty reasons to provide people with enough of some good, whether it is wealth, health or, in our case, autonomy through education, and that some of these reasons do not apply once we have secured enough. This changes the reasons we can offer in support of claims for more of that good. In this case the shift helps us to distinguish the extent of autonomy that is most important from the further improvements in autonomy, which may still be weighty, and weightier than a parent's interest in removing his or her child from some education, but are less important. The shift highlights that we have stronger reasons to resist sacrifices in sufficient autonomy than to resist further improvements.

The sufficientarian principle draws our attention to why autonomy is valued. Instrumental arguments claim that autonomy is valued because it helps us to live better lives. Sometimes this is true, but in the case of the traditional community, we have grounds to think that this is not true. I claim that autonomy is valued because it is important for our freedom and that once we have secured enough, other reasons, including instrumental reasons, become relatively more significant in debates about whether we should promote it further.

The sufficientarian approach helps us to see how we might make a principled compromise or at least frame a public debate. It helps us to understand this debate in the following way. Whoever is correct about the instrumental benefits of education for autonomy, we have weighty reasons to provide people with enough education to be free. This, I have argued, requires deliberation, a disposition to exchange reasons with others in a tolerant and civil manner, and it requires information and knowledge both of oneself and of the external world. Anything associated with education for autonomy that is not to do with realising the conditions of freedom must be supported by a different profile of reasons. So, even if the traditional communities are correct about the damaging effects of education for autonomy on their children's welfare, there is something further to say about autonomy's value as a part of freedom. We have something to say about certain specific educational topics. They may more easily opt out of other topics on grounds of well-being, but they may not opt out of this so easily.

In democratic societies this sufficientarian approach has some advantages. The shift enables us to find a principled compromise, which may be an improvement that is achievable through democratic means. Note that arguments for the instrumental value of autonomy have emphasised not only critical reasoning skills as a reliable guide to living well, but also the democratic skills required for democratic decision-making and being well informed about matters of policy. This, it has been claimed, includes having an adequate knowledge of science and world history and an ability to analyse and assess policy arguments.[6] However, it is harder to justify these skills of autonomy when they are not linked to the conditions of freedom. Our main concern with a lack knowledge of basic science, world history and awareness of various policy arguments is that it would raise questions about the freedom with which individuals' views were held. Individuals would be denied important evidential bases on which to form their beliefs. Emphasis on other requirements, such as jury service, seems to be beside the point with respect to some of our strongest reasons and it seems that an opt-out could more easily be justified. Of course, there may be good reasons to ensure that everyone has such knowledge but the case for it must be made on different grounds. Instead, our insistence on the conditions of freedom highlights that critical reasoning is important and that education for autonomy intended to ensure that we hold our beliefs freely is much harder to opt out of than classes on jury service and good citizenship in the ways understood above.

Moreover, it seems that the lack of freedom, in itself, is what disturbs most of those who consider education for autonomy to be compulsory. It is the thought that those in Amish communities have never had the opportunity to revise their views and their values that disturbs us and not the fact that their lives could be better if they became liberal democrats. The disturbing thought is that Amish children will not be brought up under the conditions of freedom, and so do not come to believe freely. It is not that they cannot live flourishing lives within that community.

An advantage of the sufficientarian non-instrumental approach to the practical debate is that it provides us with guidance tailored to our reasons. Some aspects of autonomy are not as important as others and the arguments from those in religious communities to opt out more easily succeed in outweighing some aspects of autonomy than others. In particular, the aspects that are most important for well-being may not be the same as those that are most important for freedom. Thus, the sufficientarian standard provides us with helpful guidance when assessing requests to exempt children from certain kinds of education: to provide an education that would convince an impartial spectator or hypothetically contracting party that whatever their beliefs, they were formed freely.

In this section I have shown that the principle of sufficient autonomy has important implications for one important debate about education for autonomy. I have argued that sufficientarian principles can help us to frame the debate in terms of the kinds of education that can be opted out of more easily than others and I have argued that a non-instrumental argument has advantages over an instrumental argument in both theoretical and practical aspects of this practical debate. This bodes well for the prospects for sufficientarianism.

The Implications of the Principle of Sufficient Autonomy

Before I go on to explain the other contributions that the principle of sufficient autonomy has for debates about education, I will set out the principle again and its implications for education. The principle of sufficient autonomy states that as part of the conditions of freedom individuals should be sufficiently autonomous. I have said that this means that it is especially important that all individuals be able to give reasons for their views and be able and willing to deliberate with others. Moreover, their deliberation must be informed.

I believe that the principle of sufficient autonomy has three main implications for educational institutions, and these implications set aims for educational institutions which are not easily outweighed by other concerns because the conditions of freedom are a weighty requirement of justice.

Deliberative Powers

The first implication of the principle of sufficient autonomy is that individuals must have an awareness of their own reasoning to their own views and what we might think of as basic reasoning skills; they must be familiar with fallacies of argument and rhetorical ploys. The appropriate education will depend upon the fallacies and rhetoric that are being used in society and the importance of being aware of some devices varies relative to the frequency with which they are used. These skills are necessary to participate in a meaningful deliberative process, the preconditions of which are required to ensure they believe freely. These deliberative powers will help individuals to resist bad arguments and also to make use of opportunities to deliberate with others.

Disposition

The second implication is that individuals must obtain a disposition to participate in deliberation with others. To do so individuals must be acquainted with deliberative reasoning from an early age and this disposition will more likely be acquired if a tolerant atmosphere and background conditions of civil argument and debate are cultivated and maintained. This requires a certain degree of self-confidence, which must come from encouragement in debate and deliberation too. Even if a person has deliberative powers, failing to engage with others can affect our ability to see what is wrong with our own plans and deprives us of the assurance that comes from considering alternative points of view and alternative plans of life. Only when one has a disposition to engage in discussion with those one disagrees with can one's plan be freely held. If we do not seek to engage in argument those with whom we disagree, then we deprive ourselves of reasonable assurance, not of truth, of free belief.

Talents Discovery

The third implication of the principle of sufficient autonomy for education is that individuals must be well informed about the options open to them. Since our judgements about the value of some choice often depend upon our familiarity with that practice and our knowledge of our talents, I propose a requirement regarding the discovery of talents derived from the principle of sufficient autonomy. This requirement states that individuals should have a good idea of where their interests and natural talents lie. This partly constitutes the conditions of freedom since, when one is deprived of a variety of experiences that will reveal a spread of talents and interests, one is deprived of the opportunity to make informed decisions about what one's life will be like. While it would doubtless be costly, and inappropriate, to require individuals to attempt all opportunities, or to maximise the amount of opportunity given, it is plausible to think that some variety of opportunities to discover one's talents is required for sufficient autonomy. I will say more in defence of this later.

The implication for educational institutions is, I believe, that schools, as the most well-suited institutions for this purpose, should provide a comprehensive education where children are encouraged to try a range of activities rather than to focus on a narrow few. Perhaps we can say that the practical aim is to design provision of education such that, upon graduation, students have experienced a variety of disciplines (academic, artistic and sporting) and have a good idea of what their interests are and where their abilities lie. If not, then that intrinsically important part of their freedom is likely infringed. Their ability to freely and competently set targets for themselves is diminished. This kind of self-knowledge is important if one is going to choose for oneself. This is because our choices about what to pursue are deeply affected by our likely success and our past acquaintance with that practice. The freedom of individuals rests on their being informed in these matters, which rests on their being allowed and encouraged, and perhaps being forced in some cases, to pursue various tasks that will help them to discover their interests and talents.

A variety of exercises and activities should be compulsory for some time, since often we do not have a good idea of what we are good at or interested in until we have experienced a number of different disciplines in a number of different contexts at a number of stages in our development. Over time students should be able to focus on those disciplines they find most interesting or enjoyable. I shall term the implication that states 'everyone should be given opportunities sufficient to discover their talents and interests insofar as this constitutes our freedom as sufficiently autonomous agents' the 'requirement of talents discovery'. Critics will claim that breadth requirements should be weighed up against depth of knowledge and talent development, and they are right. However, insofar as we have very weighty reasons to be concerned with sufficient autonomy, and breadth is supported by that value, a measure of breadth is going to be a key demand of justice in education.

Having clarified what I take to be the main implications of the principle of sufficient autonomy for education, I will now show that the principle and its implications should have an extensive role in our thought. I focus on this third and perhaps least familiar implication as it has important implications for a commonly discussed account of equality of opportunity in education: fair equality of opportunity. I will first show that the requirement of talents discovery makes the principle of fair equality of opportunity more coherent and plausible and I will then show that it enables proponents of that principle to defend themselves against an otherwise compelling objection. Both points I make will illustrate the contribution that the principle of sufficient autonomy can make regarding the well-known and much discussed principle of fair equality of opportunity and as such show that sufficient autonomy should have an extensive role in our thought.

Fair Equality of Opportunity

Rawls's principle of fair equality of opportunity is a prominent view about justice that has implications for educational provision.[7] The principle requires that careers be open to talents on a competitive basis. This means that jobs should be awarded to the best-qualified applicant for that particular position. Careers being open to talents requires that public offices and social positions be, at least formally, open to all. The competition referred to here is meritocratic. It requires that successful applicants be appointed in virtue, and solely in virtue, of their ability to do the job well. In addition to this, fair equality of opportunity requires that all have a fair chance to attain these offices and positions, or in other words, everyone must have a fair chance to be the victor in the meritocratic competition for jobs.[8] Everyone has a fair chance to be the victor in competitions for jobs, Rawls claims, when those with the same native talents and motivation have the same prospects for success in the attainment of public offices and social positions, regardless of their social background.[9] However, inequalities in opportunity are permitted so long as they are to the benefit of the least advantaged.[10] For my current purposes the most interesting claim that the principle of fair equality of opportunity makes is that education should be distributed to preserve this fair chances condition. I now spell out that condition before showing that, in order to be more complete and more plausible, this view must be supplemented with the *requirement of talents discovery*.

Rawls's definition of fair chances requires that those with the same talents and motivation have the same prospects of success in pursuit of jobs.[11] Whether an arrangement is just, then, turns on whether the equally talented and motivated are equal in their 'prospects for success' in the attainment of offices and positions. Since educational provision often affects how far our native talents are developed, and since how far our native talents are developed affects our prospects for success in pursuit of jobs, education has an essential role in preserving the fair chances condition. To clarify what this means we need to know what is meant by talents and motivation and the sense in which they can be equal. We also need to establish the most plausible reading of 'prospects for success in the pursuit of jobs' and how two people might be equal in this respect. I will argue that reflecting on these terms reveals a problem with the principle of fair equality of opportunity, but this problem can be solved by supplementing it with the requirement of talents discovery, derived from the principle of sufficient opportunity.

'Talent' can mean a variety of things including a skill that an individual has without having worked at it, the potential to develop some skill easily, the potential to develop that skill to a high degree, or a skill or ability that has been developed over time. The plausibility of the principle of fair equality of opportunity varies depending on the interpretation of talent used, so it is important to resolve this ambiguity.

Rawls sometimes writes of the 'distribution of native endowments' and it is easy to see why when we consider that he thought that one's social class of origin should not affect one's prospects for success relative to others.[12] Rawls's focus on talents as native endowments can be explained by reference to the effect social class has on the opportunity we get to develop talent. If we take developed talents rather than native talents as our interpretation of talents, then we end up justifying the vast inequalities that exist due to social class, which Rawls clearly thinks are unjust. So the idea is that, given that there is some distribution of natural talents or native endowments, those with the same native talents should be in the same cohort if they also have the same level of ambition or motivation. If we could not properly specify such levels, then there may not be anything we can speak of as equal talents for the purposes of justice and this would devastate the principle of fair opportunity. So we must look to at least further specify the principle.

Attempts to further specify the principle of fair equality of opportunity, however, raise a particular problem and this leaves open further questions about the obviousness of our natural talents and the lengths to which we should go to reveal talents that may be hidden and would otherwise remain undeveloped. This is where I believe the requirement of talents discovery plays an important role in fitting into, and rendering more complete, the principle of fair equality of opportunity.

In response to the question 'Which talents are to count in the determination of your cohort?' we could say that all talents, known and unknown, count. But, since motivation and willingness to develop these talents requires their being known, these talents need not be developed at all consistent with fair equality of opportunity. It is implausible to require those with the same talents and motivation to have the same prospects for success when these talents are completely unknown. Our likelihood of developing talent-sensitive ambitions is affected by the level of development of our talents. Because of this objection, we should dismiss this 'all-talents' response to the question.

Another response would be to say that only talents that become known are to count in the determination of cohort membership. However, this view could have terribly counter-intuitive consequences if we do not supplement it with a requirement to discover talents to a certain extent. If we only count known talents in the determination of cohort membership, then this could excuse extreme class-based inequalities where wealthy parents spend more resources than poorer parents on making their children's talents known. If there is no programme for discovery of talents, then very few individuals could expect to be members of what we would intuitively think of as the correct cohort for them. Fair equality of opportunity needs to be supplemented by a principle that can tell us how to devote resources to people to make talents known.

The difficulty of identifying what is meant by talents in order to put individuals into the correct cohort for comparison is not merely an epistemic one. If the problem was merely that it is difficult to *know* who has what talents, we could just say that in practice we need to use the best proxy. But this will not do in our case because problems of justice in the distribution of benefits and burdens are raised by considering what our best is, and, indeed, if we should do our best for some or all, or if we should instead secure enough. Thus, the following question is an important one: 'How should opportunity for the development of knowledge of our talents be distributed?'

To attempt to fully reveal all of the talents of all individuals would place a huge burden on education systems. It is implausible to think that education systems, or indeed the just society, are required to discover, and develop, any talent anyone may have however expensive and however well hidden. For example, it is possible that given adequate training and encouragement Amy would have been a rather good cricketer, especially had her school picked up on this at an early age. However, her school spent more time attempting to cultivate any rugby-playing ability she had, which was already somewhat obvious or cheaper to develop by that time. If the school, or society more generally, had recognised her potential, which was not manifest, for cricket and had instead given her fairly minimal training, then she could have had an opportunity to take it further and may have been an excellent cricketer. Then she could have made informed decisions about whether to develop that talent further and whether to add cricket to one of her hobbies and ambitions that would contribute to her well-being. I doubt that this is an injustice if Amy had adequate scope for the development of her other potentials and, although regrettable for Amy, it is not an injustice because she was good at other things and those talents were developed, even though this ultimately lowered her prospects for success. On the other hand, if she did not receive any development of talents in the area of sports or recreational activities, it may have been an injustice as it would have affected her ability to determine her ambitions and preferences freely.

I believe the most plausible way to respond to the problem of making talents known is to offer to all a variety of exercises known to reveal a good spread of talents. If, however, some children did not develop talents from this range of activities, educational institutions should spend more time searching for ways to develop or reveal their talents by giving them more opportunity and resources so that they may realise the good of developing their talents. Given adequate conditions under which a good spread of natural talents can become known, fair equality of opportunity requires that those with the same known talents have the same prospects for success in the pursuit of positions. Any plausible principle of justice applying to education must take this adequacy view of the discovery of talents seriously or else it will treat those with known talents and those with unknown talents the same or provide no imperative to treat people fairly in the discovery of their talents. This innovation strengthens the case for a role for sufficientarianism in thinking about justice in education and shows that the requirement of talent discovery fits in well with other demands.

There may, of course, be additional reasons of justice to be concerned about inequalities above the threshold. If children from wealthier backgrounds received far more resources to facilitate talent discovery than children from poor backgrounds, we might find this objectionable too, but the grounds on which we would make this objection would have to be different from those offered by the principle of sufficient autonomy. Here I have only sought to show that it is especially important that we devote sufficient resources to talents discovery. I have not made the claim, associated with upper limit sufficientarianism, that inequalities above the threshold are not disturbing from the point of view of justice. This helps us to clarify and render more coherent the principle of fair equality of opportunity and strengthens the claim that the prospects for sufficientarianism are good and better than has been thought.

Arneson's Objection

In addition to clarifying the extent to which we should go to make talents known, the requirement of talents discovery can help to resolve a further problem that threatens to undermine the principle of fair equality of opportunity even in this stronger form. Richard Arneson has argued that it is not plausible to think that offices and positions conferring advantages are special distribuenda such that they should have their own distributive principle, as they do in Rawls's theory. Arneson's own considered position is that distributive justice should be concerned with well-being and that offices and positions, and social and economic goods, are reducible to their contribution to well-being. Since they can be so reduced, he claims, we should have a single distributive principle for well-being. His preferred view is that we should be prioritarians about well-being.[13]

Arneson observes that:

> The only comment Rawls makes that supports the priority of Fair Equality over the Difference Principle appeals to the point that Fair

Equality regulates the distribution of goods that may be more important to human fulfilment than the social and economic benefits regulated by the Difference Principle.[14]

In Rawls's words:

> If some places were not open on a fair basis to all, those kept out
> would be right in feeling unjustly treated even though they benefited
> from the greater efforts of those who were allowed to hold them.
> They would be justified in their complaint not only because they were
> excluded from certain external rewards of office, but because they
> were debarred from experiencing the realization of self which comes
> from a skilful and devoted exercise of social duties. They would be
> deprived of one of the main forms of human good.[15]

Arneson's challenge to Rawls unfolds in two parts. First, Arneson
argues that:

> Within Rawls' theory, which eschews any social evaluation of peo-
> ple's conceptions of the good, there does not seem to be a basis for
> affirming that the goods of job satisfaction and meaningful work
> trump the goods that money and resources distributed by the differ-
> ence principle can obtain. From the different perspectives afforded
> by different and conflicting conceptions of the good, individuals will
> differ on this question. So it will not suit Rawls to argue for the prior-
> ity of Fair Equality by appealing to the superiority of the human goods
> associated with job satisfaction.[16]

This part of the challenge requires that any justification of the
principle of fair equality of opportunity must not make a social
evaluation of people's conceptions of the good. It must remain, in
the spirit of Rawls's theory, neutral on such questions.

Second, Arneson argues that even if realisation of the self is
special:

> This premise does not support Fair Equality, but rather the inclusion
> of the goods of authority and responsibility within the scope of the
> difference principle, with extra weight attached to these goods in an

index of primary social goods that measures an individual's condition for the purposes of determining if they are justly treated.[17]

In other words, even if self-realisation linked to jobs is an especially important part of well-being, it can be accommodated within the currency of well-being itself. Positions and offices sometimes play an important part in flourishing human lives. Many people strongly identify with their work, but sometimes they do not and compromise by doing a job they do not enjoy so that they can spend more leisure time or resources on non-work-based projects. So, in the fundamental expression of our principles of distributive justice our concern should be with flourishing or well-being. This view directs us to benefit individuals in terms of jobs when jobs will improve their well-being and to benefit them in other ways when jobs will not improve their well-being. It seems to provide us with the correct answer in both cases. Putting this together, the challenge for defenders of fair equality of opportunity is to show that there is an argument for the special importance of self-realisation that:

1. does not rely upon social evaluations of the good life; and
2. explains the importance of self-realisation for justice such that it cannot be reduced solely to its contribution to well-being.

I believe that the principle of sufficient autonomy and the requirement of talents discovery provide us with such an argument.

A Sufficientarian Response

To provide a response to Arneson's challenge I draw on the value of self-realisation derived from the requirement of talents discovery. Since this commitment to autonomy is independent of its contribution to well-being and does not require a social evaluation of conceptions of the good, we should be able to construct a defence of the revised principle of fair equality of opportunity and its focus on realisation of self that satisfies the two criteria mentioned above.

I have argued that justice requires sufficient autonomy, and one element of sufficient autonomy is that individuals should have a good idea of where their talents and interests lie. Assuming a distribution of natural talents, as Rawls does, talents can go easily unnoticed. It is important that individuals understand both the extent and kind of talents they have, not only because it will make it easier for them to contribute to their own well-being – it may not – but because it enables them to make informed decisions about the revision and rational pursuit of their conception of the good, which is central to the conditions of freedom. Indeed, it is hard to imagine someone sensibly refining their conception of the good and autonomously pursuing it without such knowledge. Consider the example of a person who believes that he is no good at cricket when in reality he only believes so because the physical education teacher was instructing him to bat/bowl right-handed and he is left-handed. This person has not only been cheated of a possibly important source of well-being but has also been cheated in a further way which violates his autonomy and the conditions of freedom, at least if he has not discovered other talents. A different example that illustrates this point is that some schools may not teach a wide range of subjects, opting instead for specialisation. However, if one's schooling focusses wholly on scientific subjects and not on the arts, or vice versa, one is deprived of knowledge of one's possible talents in other areas and is therefore deprived of that knowledge of one's talents and interests that is required for the conditions of freedom. The point is merely to illustrate that such a narrow education can amount to a violation of one's freedom constituting an injustice.

There is an injustice in denying individuals knowledge of their talents by arranging society so that their well-being, understood in Arneson's terms, is higher. This autonomy requires that their natural talents are developed to a certain degree, and that realisation of the self is required to at least a sufficient level. Only when we have developed our talents to a certain level do we really have a good idea about what our talents are, the extent of such talents, and whether we enjoy exercising them. So, even if we had technology that could profile our native talents, we would still need sufficient self-realisation to make autonomous decisions about which to develop because we would not have prior knowledge of the enjoyment we derive from exercising the talents we have.

In addition to having a certain kind of education the requirement of sufficient self-realisation requires that no one be denied access to offices and social positions on any grounds other than that, after sufficient opportunity, no talents were found. As such, self-realisation is a special type of good since it constitutes autonomy required to secure our status as free and equal moral persons, which for Rawls is valuable independent of its contribution to well-being. Thus, there is an argument from Rawls that can justify the special contribution self-realisation makes that is independent of its contribution to well-being and therefore without making social evaluations of conceptions of the good life.

Of course, opponents of the principle could contest this account of the non-instrumental value of autonomy, but in flagging up this Rawlsian response we can see that those who object in the way that Arneson has must apply pressure elsewhere. Applying such pressure to autonomy will be more difficult, I believe, because it is less plausible to say that autonomy is only instrumentally valuable than it is to say that the special goods related to jobs are not reducible to well-being.

The requirement of talents discovery enables us to resolve two important problems with the principle of fair equality of opportunity. The first problem was that the principle did not seem to have any requirement applying to the lengths we should go to in order to make talents known. The requirement of talents discovery completes this task. The second problem was that Arneson points out that there are no grounds for the principle because there is no reason to think that self-realisation is special relative to other social goods without appealing to premises Rawls himself rejects. The principle of sufficient autonomy, and the requirement of talents discovery, clarifies the relationship between self-realisation, education and autonomy. Thus, we have seen that the principle of sufficient autonomy fits well with the existing demands of justice in education and helps to resolve some problems. I shall now argue that the role I find for considerations of sufficiency in an account of educational justice is more plausible than the role that has been advocated in the past.

The Place of Sufficiency in Education

It has been argued that there is a place for sufficientarianism in debates about justice in the provision of education. As a demand of justice in education, sufficiency is typically conceptualised in terms of adequacy. There are several roles that an adequacy threshold can play in a full account of justice in education. Some adequacy theorists claim that their conception of adequacy is the sole principle of justice in this area.[18] Others suggest that adequacy and equality can be used together for a full account of justice in education.[19] I will now show that the two main attempts to develop a sufficientarian standard of justice in education are less plausible than the role I find for considerations of sufficiency because they make the familiar mistakes associated with sufficientarianism that were discussed in Chapter 1. Thus, I conclude that we should be more optimistic about prospects for sufficientarianism than we have previously had reason to be.

Anderson's Fair Opportunity in Education

Elizabeth Anderson claims that justice in education requires a fair opportunity for all. The meaning of a fair opportunity for all is given by a particular adequacy threshold based on the education sufficient to produce an effective democratic elite. Anderson defines elites as 'those who occupy positions of responsibility and leadership in society: managers, consultants, professionals, politicians, policy makers'.[20] The idea is that because elites exercise greater influence on society than other 'non-elites', it is important that these elites receive a certain kind of education.

Fair opportunity in education sets a level of achievement over and above which, Anderson claims, inequalities do not matter.[21] This threshold is presented as the sole principle of justice in education. To derive the content of an adequate education Anderson describes an ideal conception of a democratic 'elite' and then claims that education must be distributed to achieve this composition. This requires that elite membership be composed along all lines of social inequality, meaning that the elite must have representatives from the different groups in society and not merely at token levels.[22] This is important because an elite composed solely of those from the same background, say wealthy, private school educated, white men, is likely to lack knowledge of the interests of those they serve, including working-class Muslim women living in rural areas, and is likely to lack a disposition to serve them. Members of the elite are likely to stereotype those they do not know and so miscalculate their interests. The cognitive deficits Anderson associates with unqualified elites worsen the position of the least advantaged in society and minority groups by enacting and creating ill-informed policy. Whether the elite are well qualified and well constituted or ill qualified and ill constituted has far-reaching effects on the lives of all in a democracy and so we all have an interest in having a well-qualified elite. Anderson explains the role of elites in the following passage:

> In a democratic society, elites must be so constituted that they will effectively serve all sectors of society, not just themselves. They must perform in their offices so that the inequalities in power, autonomy, responsibility, and reward they enjoy in virtue of their position redound to the benefit of all, including the least advantaged. This requires that elites be so constituted as to be systematically responsive to the interests and concerns of people from all walks of life.[23]

Anderson gives four qualifications that will enable and dispose the elite to be responsive to, and effectively serve the interests of, people from all sectors of society. These qualifications are the basis for her conception of adequacy. The first two qualifications are intended to make the elite responsive to the interests of people from all sectors of society. These are: (1) an awareness of the interests and problems of people from all sectors of society and (2) a disposition to serve those interests.[24] The third and fourth qualifications are to aid elites in effectively serving those interests. These are: (3) technical knowledge of how to advance these interests and (4) competence in respectful interaction with people from all sectors of society.[25] Anderson claims that an elite must be diversely constituted in order to possess the requisite knowledge.[26] This restricts the positional advantages that can be bought by extra education, since private schooling, for example, only promotes better academic qualifications, which is only part of one of these qualifications.[27] An educational system is adequate, in her view, when it educates people so that the elite are responsive and effective.

It is often thought that sufficientarian views, usually concerned with non-comparative facts, cannot deal with the injustice of positional advantages such as those linked to education.[28] Education, it is claimed, is a positional good since some of its benefits are conferred relative to one's position in the distribution of education and not the absolute level achieved. For example, those applicants with the best qualifications tend to get job interviews. An alleged advantage of Anderson's account of adequacy is that it permits those parents who value extra academic education, and want to send their children to a private school, to purchase it without causing unfairness through inadequacy. This private schooling will allow parents to give expression to their own views or satisfy their children's preference for a better academic education without also unfairly assisting their own children in the pursuit of the best jobs. Thus, it seems that we can, if we hold this sufficientarian view of justice in education, make parental partiality and fairness compatible.

There is still the problem of the residual positional advantages from within-group competition. The richest parents can secure greater shares of educational resources for their children than others and thus increase the likelihood of their children entering the elite. There seems to be some residual unfairness involved in the richest in the cohort typically becoming members of the elite. However, we might think this is so weak that it does not challenge the adequacy view. This could be because it does not reinforce social stigma and would break down the worst kinds of unfairness, such as inequalities in race and class.

However, the way that Anderson restricts positional advantages is by claiming that an elite must be representative of all of the different social groups in society. A diverse group will better fulfil the qualifications required for an effective elite. Coming from a certain social or ethnic background will therefore count as part of what qualifies a person for elite membership. However, since an adequate education is defined as qualification for elite membership, her view is consistent with providing some groups in society with an inferior academic education. Members of these groups could therefore lack part of the academic qualification and still be qualified for elite membership on the basis of their ethnic or social group because of the relative weight of their group membership. Clearly, the view should not permit this sort of injustice but, as stated, the view is consistent with it. If we really care about qualifying all for elite membership, then we need not distribute many resources to some minority groups because the diverse composition requirement means that they will qualify whatever their level of education. Minorities, qua minorities, possess a sufficient qualification for elite membership regardless of their developed talents. Part of what qualifies persons for elite membership is their ethnic or social background, due to the composition requirement, and so this view is consistent with a much lower level of investment in those born-qualified groups.

To the extent that Anderson abandons these factors (socioeconomic and cultural background) as qualifications she allows in the cognitive deficits she objects to and she enhances the relative importance of academic qualification in reaching the threshold. This greatly enhances the positional advantages that can be purchased through private education beyond within-group competition. Moreover, as private enterprises, private schools would presumably change their curriculum and composition so as to qualify their students for an elite position. This could occur by focussing on group integration, bringing about the positive disposition to serve the interests of all in society or by focussing on competence in communication with different groups. All of these could be better achieved in better-funded private schools or businesses than in worse-funded state schools. To avoid this we would have to abandon allowing private education or private businesses to sell qualifications as a commodity. This move, however, would render the view no longer advantageous in terms of permitting those who value additional academic qualifications and would look remarkably similar to an equality view and so would no longer be distinctive.

Two further problems that an adequacy threshold faces are

mentioned by Brighouse and Swift in their reply to Anderson and Satz.[29] These common problems for thresholds were also expressed by Paula Casal and were noted in Chapter 1 in their most general form.[30] Above the threshold Anderson's view is silent about the distribution of educational resources, although it seems fairly clear that there are still better and worse ways of distributing them, for example, to enhance the prospects of those with the worst prospects. Her view is a version of upper limit sufficientarianism and, as I have shown in Chapter 1, as a version of upper limit sufficientarianism it is vulnerable to the indifference objection. Further inequalities, once adequacy is achieved, do seem to matter because academic education confers positional advantages but Anderson's account cannot condemn these inequalities.

To conclude, Anderson's adequacy threshold picks out something important, which is the good that educated people can do for the less well educated in positions of leadership and responsibility. This may improve the position of the least well off and all in society. However, this cannot be the whole story. Above the threshold positional advantages need to be limited or we need some explanation of why they are justified. Anderson attempts the former but at the cost of being caught by a dilemma. Anderson either mitigates positional advantage leaving open the possibility of a lower threshold for minorities, or she removes ethnic and social status as qualifications for elite membership and allows the wealthy to buy positional advantages.

Satz's Educational Adequacy

I shall now expound Debra Satz's conception of educational adequacy and show that it is also less plausible than the principle of sufficient autonomy as a sufficientarian demand of justice in education because it is vulnerable to familiar objections to sufficientarianism.

For Satz educational adequacy is tied to full citizenship and so inequalities in educational opportunity are constrained by the requirements of full citizenship. This is to say that inequalities are unjustified if they alter the status of any citizen to second class or less than full citizenship. However, all inequalities that do not violate this constraint are permissible as long as adequacy is achieved for all who can achieve it. Like Anderson, Satz seems to provide a version of upper limit sufficientarianism.

Satz's view ties educational adequacy to the requirements of equal citizenship.[31] Her view is related to the desirable civic purposes that a conception of educational adequacy may serve. Satz's view retains relational elements in her conception of adequate education.[32] Satz's conception of educational adequacy is focussed on the substance of educational outcomes and institutional structure of education rather than opportunity and funding. She claims that we can derive 'the nature and content of educational adequacy from the requirements for full membership and inclusion in a democratic society of equal citizens'.[33] Satz focusses on the kind of citizens that we have reason to want to come out of the education system and this dictates the content of the threshold. This is similar to Anderson's view in that it sees the realisation of a particular social condition as the aim of education. For Satz these social conditions are full membership and inclusion.

In order to specify the adequacy threshold, Satz offers an account of a citizen by describing four important features of an ideal citizen. Citizens (1) have equal basic political rights and freedoms, including rights to speech and participation in the political process, (2) have equal rights and freedoms within civil society, including rights to own property and to justice, (3) have equal rights to a threshold of economic welfare, and (4) have equal rights to 'share to the full in the social heritage and to live the life of a civilized being according to the standards prevailing in the society'.[34] I call these features 'citizenship capabilities'.

Satz then proceeds to derive the requirements for adequacy in education from these 'citizenship capabilities'. The first feature requires a level of knowledge and competence in using the rights and freedoms with which each citizen should be endowed. This includes basic freedoms, such as freedom of speech, but also the freedom to participate in politics and the economy. The specific level depends on the social context.[35] To meet the threshold citizens must also possess competence in group interaction to promote mutual respect and tolerance.[36] This, she suggests, can be achieved through the diverse composition of schools. Although some inequality in opportunity is tolerated, her conception of adequacy constrains these inequalities. Unacceptable inequalities in opportunity arise when some citizens are effectively ruled out of some social positions or are viewed as second-class citizens.[37]

The account of adequacy presented is one for full and equal citizenship. Justice is done so long as everyone has the requisite knowledge and competence to make use of their rights and freedoms, can actively engage in political and economic roles as formulated for their particular social context and achieve competence in social interaction, and resulting inequalities are not so severe as to create second-class citizens. Satz's account of adequacy focusses on the satiable aims set by each of the citizenship capabilities and this provides us with an absolute level, that of full citizenship, but it can also eradicate worries we might have about relative differences, such as the social stigma attached to 'second-class' citizens.

'Citizenship capabilities' are no doubt important capabilities and ones that an education system can encourage and help to develop. However, this cannot be a full account of justice in education. The value of the capability to exercise freedoms and rights depends partly on the development of various personal interests. If we imagine Satz's threshold is met and the distribution of education also meets her 'no second-class citizens' constraint, then we have citizens who can use their rights, are qualified for economic participation and know how to vote, etc. Without development of personal interests the value of these rights is diminished and so this version of adequacy cannot be the sole principle for the distribution of education.

We should also bear in mind debates about traditional communities and education discussed in this chapter. Satz's account would require that traditional communities allow their children to stay at school so that they can learn about political institutions and jury service, among other things. These are much less compelling reasons than the reason of freedom to form one's beliefs.

Citizenship capabilities are important. They correspond to the duties placed on individuals as citizens. It seems that there is at least some onus on the state to equip citizens with the skills required to perform jury service, for example. But this cannot be the whole justification and point of education. Likewise, we all have an interest in there being as many good citizens as possible because it is better to share our political community with good rather than bad citizens. Certainly, these goals have some plausibility. However, due to the number and strength of objections we can make of Anderson's and Satz's sufficientarian views that cannot be made of the principle of sufficient autonomy, we can see that the latter yields a significant improvement in the prospects for sufficientarianism in educational debates.

Conclusion

In this chapter I have argued that the principle of sufficient autonomy, defended in the previous chapter, should have an extensive role in our thought. I did so by showing that the principle has important implications for the design of education policy, that it has important implications for a debate about the place of autonomy in education provision, and that one implication, regarding talents discovery, fits well with fair equality of opportunity and helps it to avoid a powerful objection. Thus, I have argued that the prospects for sufficientarianism seem to be good because there is an indispensable sufficientarian principle which should have an extensive role in our thought about practical debates. This supports optimism about the prospects for sufficientarianism.

In the next chapter I will extend my re-examination of sufficientarianism by showing that sufficientarian principles may be more plausible than their rivals where there are value clashes. I defend a principle of the good enough upbringing and argue that this principle should have an extensive role in our thought also.

Notes

1. *Wisconsin v. Yoder*, 406 US 205 – Supreme Court (1972).
2. In ibid., the judge states that, 'Amish objection to formal education beyond the eighth grade is firmly grounded in these central

religious concepts. They object to the high school and higher education generally, because the values they teach are in marked variance with Amish values and the Amish way of life; they view secondary school education as an impermissible exposure of their children to a "worldly" influence in conflict with their beliefs. The high school tends to emphasise intellectual and scientific accomplishments, self-distinction, competitiveness, worldly success, and social life with other students. Amish society emphasises informal learning-through-doing; a life of "goodness," rather than a life of intellect; wisdom, rather than technical knowledge; community welfare, rather than competition; and separation from, rather than integration with, contemporary worldly society.'

3. Brighouse and Swift, 'Legitimate parental partiality'.
4. Ibid., 59–64.
5. In Arneson and Shapiro, 'Democratic autonomy and religious liberty', 399–400, the authors state that 'Insofar as critical reflection on one's present values is a useful means to acquiring values that could withstand informed critical reflection and that would be a reliable guide to a valuable and worthy life, one's basic goal of living a good life generates the subsidiary goal of developing and exercising critical reflection. This, as we have seen, is the core defensible aspect of the ideal of autonomy.'
6. Ibid., 376.
7. This part of the chapter is based in part on Shields, 'From Rawlsian autonomy to sufficient opportunity in education'.
8. In Rawls, *Justice as Fairness*, 43, the author states that 'Fair equality of opportunity is said to require not merely that public offices and social positions be open in the formal sense, but that all should have a fair chance to attain them.'
9. In ibid., 44, the author states that 'To specify the idea of a fair chance we say: supposing that there is a distribution of native endowments, those with the same level of talents and ability and the same willingness to use those gifts should have the same prospects of success regardless of their social class of origin, the class into which they are born and develop until the age of reason.'
10. In Rawls, *A Theory of Justice*, 266, the author states that 'an inequality in opportunity must enhance the opportunity of those with the lesser opportunity'.
11. Ibid., 44.
12. Ibid., 44.
13. In Arneson, 'Against Rawlsian equality of opportunity', 97, the

author states: 'My own view is that foundational principles of justice should be responsive to the quality of lives that people would be enabled to lead by proposed social policies rather than to the amount of resources they are enabled to get.'

14. Ibid., 97.
15. Rawls, *A Theory of Justice*, 73.
16. Arneson, 'Against Rawlsian equality of opportunity', 98.
17. Ibid., 98–9.
18. Anderson, 'Fair opportunity in education'; Gutmann, *Democratic Education*; Curren, 'Justice and the threshold of educational equality'.
19. Brighouse and Swift, 'Educational equality versus educational adequacy'.
20. Anderson, 'Fair opportunity in education', 596.
21. In Anderson, 'Fair opportunity in education', 615, the author states that 'Sufficientarian principles do not constrain inequalities in educational access above the sufficiency threshold.'
22. In ibid., 617, the author states that 'If they are present in only token numbers, members of advantaged groups will have few opportunities to have significant interaction with them. Tokenism also primes group stereotypes rather than defusing them.'
23. Ibid., 596.
24. Ibid., 596.
25. Ibid., 596.
26. In ibid., 616, the author states that 'The qualifications required for a democratic elite put sharp constraints on the ability of the better-off to gain competitive advantages in this way, however. Since an elite overwhelmingly drawn from the already class-privileged is less qualified than an elite drawn from all socioeconomic classes, colleges that are doing their jobs must sharply discount the positional advantages that the prosperous can accrue by endowing their children with more academic knowledge. The marginal value to a college admissions committee of additional academic qualifications among the better-off should fall off steeply in head-to-head competition with sufficiently academically prepared students from disadvantaged social backgrounds.'
27. In ibid., 597, the author states that 'On the broader four-dimensional conception of qualification articulated above, some qualifications are essentially dispersed across all sectors of society, and others can only be developed jointly by an integrated elite. This is not to deny the relevance of academic qualifications. It is to insist

that this is a partial conception of qualification. When colleges select an elite that is truly qualified to serve everyone in society, they must select for all dimensions of qualification. This substantially reduces the positional advantages of those who are highly qualified by narrowly academic standards and grants positional advantages to those whose dispersed knowledge is relatively scarce among elites as currently constituted.'

28. Brighouse and Swift, 'Equality, priority and positional goods'.
29. Brighouse and Swift, 'Educational equality versus educational adequacy'.
30. Casal, 'Why sufficiency is not enough'.
31. Satz, 'Equality, adequacy, and education for citizenship', 625.
32. Sufficientarians usually concern themselves with absolute levels not relative levels of how well off people are, and so distance themselves from relational problems in distribution. Satz does not, and claims that some inequalities do have damaging effects and should be constrained.
33. Satz, 'Equality, adequacy, and education for citizenship', 636.
34. Ibid., 636.
35. In ibid., 636, the author states that 'First, citizenship requires a threshold level of knowledge and competence for exercising its associated rights and freedoms—liberty of speech and expression, liberty of conscience, and the right to serve on a jury, vote, and participate in politics and in the economy . . . the empirical content of this threshold itself depends on the distribution of skills and knowledge in the population as a whole.'
36. In ibid., 636, the author states that 'an education adequate for equal citizenship includes but goes beyond the achievement of a narrow list of individual skills. A society of equals is more than a collection of independent individuals but includes the ways that people cooperate and relate to one another in employment, in politics, and in making social decisions in their neighborhoods and within public spaces.'
37. In ibid., 636, the author states that 'although an adequacy standard does not insist on strictly equal opportunities for the development of children's potentials, large inequalities regarding who has a real opportunity for important goods above citizenship's threshold relegate some members of society to second-class citizenship, where they are denied effective access to positions of power and privilege in the society'.

5 A Good Enough Upbringing

In the previous two chapters I explored one strategy for defending indispensable sufficientarian principles.[1] This strategy requires us to examine whether there are any sufficientarian reasons, where sufficientarian reasons are weighty, satiable, non-egalitarian and non-instrumental. There is more work to be done if we are to thoroughly re-examine the prospects for sufficientarianism. There is at least one further general line of argument that can be used to assess the prospects for sufficientarianism and if this line of argument can be vindicated, it bodes well for the prospects for sufficientarianism. I call this the 'value clash argument'. The intuitive idea behind this line of argument is that where one value clashes with another, and both seem somewhat indispensable, the best principle to adhere to may be a principle that states that the weight of our reasons to advance a value shifts once the other value has been promoted to a sufficient extent. For example, if value A and value B seem relevant to some set of decisions and we cannot promote both, it may be best to follow the principle that states that we should promote A to a sufficient extent and then promote B. This is the alternative to simply denying that there is a value clash or giving lexical priority to one value over the other. It is also more principled than intuitively weighing each value in each case. If, as I will claim, some value clashes are most plausibly resolved by sufficientarian principles, then it seems we should be optimistic about the prospects for sufficientarianism insofar as there are such clashes.

As we have seen, certain shifts necessitate a sufficientarian principle. The sufficientarian principles supported by the value clash argument will find the middle ground between reducing one value to another, perhaps to utility or welfare, and claiming that one value has absolute priority over the other.

Leaving the value clash line of argument unexplored would leave important gaps in our understanding of the role of sufficiency in articulating the demands of distributive justice. The completion of the examination of both lines of argument will provide us with a more accurate assessment of the prospects for sufficientarianism.

In this chapter, I will use the value clash argument to defend a principle of a good enough upbringing as the correct response to a particular clash in a debate about justice and child-rearing and I will argue that this principle should have an extensive role in our thought about some important practical debates. The particular question I wish to answer is 'On what grounds can custodial parents usually be denied the right to rear?' The relevant value clash in this debate is between the child's and adult's interests. I conclude that, in respect of deciding on the custodial arrangements of a child, the child's interests have some priority over the parent's interests until they are met to a sufficient extent. Thereafter the parent's interests matter more relative to the child's interests. This yields the following guidance: so long as a parent will perform well enough with respect to the child's interests, we cannot usually remove the child from that parent's custody. No matter how good a parent is, he or she may not be totally immune from being denied custody of his or her child. The theoretical possibility of super-parents will likely yield counter-examples to any threshold claiming total immunity for a good enough parent. In light of this, I claim that there is a shift in the relative importance of the child's interests once they have been met to a sufficient extent and this supports a sufficientarian principle of distributive justice.

Negotiating this clash of values will enable us to specify and then defend a threshold level of care that is an indispensable part of a complete and sound account of justice in the distribution of child-rearing rights. I then show that this principle should have an extensive role in our thought about important practical debates.

Prospectus

In this chapter I argue for an indispensable sufficientarian principle of adequate upbringing, which governs decisions about child custody and upbringing generally by using the value clash line of argument. Specifically, I hold that an adequate upbringing is a condition attached to the right to rear and governs the reallocation of such rights. However, it is very important to notice that it alone need not govern the initial allocations of such rights. What I say in this chapter is consistent with holding many different views about adequate upbringings and biology as the bases for initially holding the child-rearing rights. My question is when those who do hold such rights can lose such rights. In order to defend this principle, I shall begin by explaining the debate I address in greater detail and will show that the debate raises problems of justice. I will then show that children should be removed from their custodial parents in at least some cases in order to protect some of the child's interests. This establishes that we require an account of the conditions attached to the right to rear and we need to answer some questions about when and why a parent can be denied custody or, in other words, when an upbringing is not 'good enough'.

The argument unfolds by considering the defects with prevailing rival approaches to this question and showing that the value clash approach to the good enough upbringing is best suited to avoiding them. I then set out and critique child-centred accounts of the distribution of the right to rear, which reject the idea of a conflict of values or interests. I do so in order to motivate a dual interest approach according to which value clashes can occur and therefore could be resolved by the value clash approach. I then consider the best-known non-sufficientarian account of the distribution of custodial rights: the best custodian view. On this view, there is no need for a sufficiency threshold since we ought to maximise the interests of the child. I argue that while this view is somewhat plausible, it is vulnerable to a powerful objection, known as the Plato Worry, which sanctions wide-scale redistribution of children from even good parents in principle. I then consider a sufficientarian but still child-centred account of the distribution of custodial rights. On this view, a child's justice-based claims regarding upbringing are themselves satiable. As such, no parent who is doing a good job can justifiably have his or her child taken away, where doing a good job meets these interests. I argue that this view is too simplistic and the actual motivation for moving away from the best custodian condition is that we care about parental interests and not that children only have satiable interests. This leads us to consider a different sort of approach, one that fits better with the value clash approach and gives independent significance to the interests of parents and children. I then set out this value clash line of argument about how to think about an adequate upbringing by contrasting it with other accounts and responding to some objections. I then show that the principle of the good enough upbringing can be properly fleshed out. To complete this task I begin by devising some desiderata and constraints that apply to an account of the good enough upbringing. I claim that a plausible account of the good enough upbringing will only make reference to the child's interests, will be satiable and will collectively account for our strongest intuitions about a good upbringing. Any candidate thresholds that meet all of these constraints will then be assessed in terms of the desiderata of how they answer the question 'How bad can a good enough parent be?' This test is given greater precision by weighing each child's interest against the adult's interest in having custody of a child. I call this the 'weight requirement'. The threshold that performs best with respect to this desideratum will be the chosen account of the good enough upbringing. I conclude with a summary and discussion of how the principle has an important role in our thought about practical debates and differs from commonly used abuse and neglect thresholds.

Child-rearing and Justice

It is a fact about most societies that some decisions about the conduct and treatment of children are not left in the hands of parents, though many are. The right to rear is the entitlement of some particular agent or agency to make some decisions with respect to a particular child. These decisions include deciding where they live, what they do with their time, their diet and their leisure activities, those familiar from the social role of parenting.

The right of some parents to rear children is certainly justified in some form because children need to be reared by someone for their own basic welfare. Moreover, it is likely to be a persistent feature of our world. As such, the question of when and why custodial parents can be denied the right to rear is important both practically and philosophically.[2] The right to rear is both limited, in that it does not allow custodians to have complete control of a child – they must act within the law, for instance – and conditional, in that custody can be removed if overridden by other concerns, but a particular agent or agency is to be responsible in the first instance for a number of important decisions regarding the life of the child.[3] This primary agent or agency holds what I call the 'right to rear'.

One peculiar feature of my specification of the right to rear is that it permits agencies, such as orphanages, and communal child-rearing institutions, such as the kibbutz, to possess the right to rear. Typically the argument that parents rather than institutions should raise children is made prior to the question of the nature, justification and scope of child-rearing rights.[4] In any case, I do not believe that my arguments turn on an eccentric understanding of the right to rear. Rather, my arguments are compatible with a number of plausible accounts of the right to rear.

Before exploring the role of sufficiency in resolving clashes of value, I must first establish that the distribution of the right to rear is a matter of justice and is not, for example, a matter of parents having pre-institutional property rights over their children, which the principles of justice must respect in order to be legitimate.[5] If this is not a debate of justice, then showing that considerations of sufficiency are pertinent to it will not promote the prospects for sufficientarianism as a position in distributive justice.

That this debate is a debate about justice can be explained as follows. Our intuitions rebel against some distributions of the right to rear and some distributions are not only aptly described as immoral but are also unjust. We should be discerning about who has the right to rear since whoever possesses it will have a profound impact upon the lives of the children in their care. To accept that distributing the right to rear is a problem of justice we only need to accept the claim that, in at least some circumstances, some people should be denied the right to rear on grounds of justice. To accept this is to accept that we should find some principled basis for such denials, which is to say, we should find an account of the distribution of the right to rear. To establish this proposition we can say that Joseph Fritzl, who repeatedly abused and raped his daughter, should not have held a right to rear.[6] Moreover, it is not merely that it would have been morally *better* if Fritzl had not had the right to rear or that someone *should* have done something to stop it. These are ethical and moral claims, but not obviously claims of justice. To clarify, we should say that society's basic institutions should be designed so as to, and insofar as is possible, systematically deprive people like Fritzl from holding the right to rear and instead allocate the right to rear to some other custodian. It is not only the case that the world is a worse place for Fritzl's having such rights, and not only is it the case that someone would have failed in some moral obligation to prevent it. The society that permits Fritzl to have such rights is unjust to the extent that it does so. The distribution of the right to rear creates problems for the just society and its institutions. As such, the idea that the family and parental rights are somehow prior to justice or insulated from it cannot be sustained insofar as it has this implication.

The only qualifying circumstances that must obtain for this proposition to be true, I believe, would be that there was an available parent who would perform better with respect to the child's interests. This qualification is required since, if the world is full of Fritzls except one other person, who will make a worse parent than Fritzl, then we should prefer Fritzl as a parent. Of course, the child may well be better off without any parents, perhaps raised by wild animals, like Mowgli from *The Jungle Book*, but I shall assume that in all relevant circumstances some adult can do better than wild animals.

I do not think that anyone would be willing to deny the claim that in some circumstances we should deny some people the right to rear as a matter of justice, even those who think that procreative parents have a *pro tanto* claim to the right to rear their children.[7] In extreme cases, like that of Fritzl, any reasonable person would agree that the *pro tanto* claim should be overridden and the child removed from the custody of his or her procreative parents. Moreover, even those who hold that we cannot know *ex ante* whether a parent will be a 'Fritzl' will agree that if we could deny him or her such a right, then we should deny him or her such a right. Therefore, they would agree that we have at least some demands of justice in this area.

The Child's Interests

Given that some criteria of justice must be used to guide and assess decisions about the distribution of the right to rear, we must now identify the most plausible criteria. The example that demonstrated that we cannot be indifferent about the distribution of child-rearing rights commits us to a constraint when devising an account of the distribution of the right to rear. Our account of the basis for decisions about the distribution of child-rearing rights should rule out Fritzls from holding them. If the account we end up with does not rule out Fritzls, then the example I gave could not provide us with a satisfactory argument to the conclusion that we cannot be indifferent about the distribution of child-rearing rights. We would have to take that necessary step again. Moreover, such an account could hardly be plausible.

When it comes to the role of the interests of the child in the distribution of child-rearing rights, there are two schools of thought. Child-centred views hold that only the child's interests are to be considered. Dual interest views hold that both the child's and the parents' interests are to be considered. It should be clear that the value clash I seek to vindicate cannot be established if the child-centred view is true because there would be no values to clash. We have already established that the child's interests are sometimes decisive in extreme circumstances. In this section I examine and argue against two child-centred views that deny there is a value clash. The first is a non-sufficientarian view that states that we should maximise the expected quality of an upbringing for a child, when determining who should have the right to rear. This is known as the best custodian condition. The second is a sufficientarian view that states that the child's relevant interests are satiable and as such, those parents who do a good enough job can rear their children even when they are not the best at promoting the child's interests. I call this the 'satiable view'. I conclude this section by rejecting the child-centred view in general. This means that we should accept a dual interest view and so we must endorse some value clash. How we resolve this clash and where we set the level of good enough parent is discussed in the following sections.

The Best Custodian Condition

Some child-centred theorists claim that the right to rear should be allocated in accordance with the best custodian condition:

> *The Best Custodian Condition*: The right to rear any child should be allocated to the interested party that is expected to fare no worse than any other interested party with respect to that child's interests.[8]

Proponents of this view, or variants of it, deny that the interests of prospective parents fundamentally matter. They also insist that the child's interests be maximised. As such, the view does not recognise a clash of interests that the sufficientarian value clash line of argument could help resolve. On the best custodian view the best parents cannot be denied the right to rear, but those who are not the best can be denied the right to rear. Importantly, on this view, we cannot force those who do not want the right to rear to have it even if they would do better for the child than any other interested party. While it seems that in some cases this may be permissible – for example, in emergency cases such as those involving the Kindertransport between 1938 and 1940, which sought to rescue Jewish children from Nazi Germany – those cases are not my focus. It also seems those kinds of cases would require a special threshold since different interests and values clash with one another. The reason for thinking that those cases would require a special threshold is that we would be overriding what some take to be a crucial liberal commitment: the adult's freedom of occupational choice.[9] An account of the good enough upbringing that must override freedom of occupational choice will require a different threshold because a different set of interests clash. I accept freedom of occupational choice, or something similar, for parents throughout my discussion and will not be discussing those types of cases, interesting though they are.

A further important thing to note about this view is that it sanctions changes in the distribution of child-rearing rights only in circumstances that are better for the child. Since instability is often very bad for children, this may mean that practically the view is quite conservative. Perhaps the most important note of caution, however, is to say that it is not an objection to this view that it will require removing children very frequently and this will have serious costs in terms of the child's interests. It simply is not supported by the principle. The principle only sanctions interference where it would benefit the child in net terms.

One can lend plausibility to the best custodian view by considering another interest that may appear to tell against it. One interest that we might think can outweigh the child's interests is society's interest in the upbringing of children. A society's population has an interest in the upbringing of children in that society. For some in society, the younger generation's having certain skills, a certain disposition to serve the older generation, or having cheaper tastes than they otherwise would, may make the lives of the older generation go better. All of these requirements are clearly inadmissible as interests relevant in determining the distribution of the right to rear in a just society where it is important that we stand as equals. To allocate the right to rear to those parents who will ensure that children they rear will have the cheapest tastes and most deferential and servile attitudes is clearly not admissible and could not outweigh the interests of the child in forming their preferences and ambitions authentically.

To illustrate this point consider a case where the best custodian condition clashes with society's interests. Imagine that there are two sets of potential parents: Alex and Ashley and Bobbie and Billie. Alex and Ashley are loving and both intend to rear their child so that the child will believe that she can achieve anything she puts her mind to. Bobbie and Billie are also loving, but they intend to rear their child so that she will believe that she should only aspire to live a life that will impose no greater costs on others than had she never been born. Whatever the merits of these two approaches to child-rearing, it is absurd to think that Bobbie and Billie should be preferred *because* they are more likely, if they are, to raise a child who will better accommodate the interests of other adults in society by having modest or stunted ambitions. If we change the example so that Bobbie and Billie will also be less loving than Alex and Ashley, and will perform less well with respect to the child's developmental interests as well, then we have even less reason to prefer them as parents. In these examples priority is rightly given to the child's interests.

We do well to note that it may be in the child's interests to be brought up in a way that makes him or her more likely to respect the claims that others have to resources. There are some relevant interests society does have in ensuring that the child does not become a resource monster who will consume a large quantity of resources thus imposing unacceptable opportunity costs on others.[10] But such interests may already be included in the requirements of justice and at least some of these – treating others in a civil manner, for example – are included in the child's interests. Insofar as individuals in society have a permissible interest in advancing their conception of a good life and in being treated fairly by others, they have an interest in the next generation being just and this constraining child-rearing practices. There may be some other ways in which the interests of third parties, that is, those who are neither parents nor children, may conflict with other relevant interests but given the prominence of interests of the child and the parents, we have reason to think they will play a secondary or tertiary role and that we can incorporate them after identifying the relationship between the interests of parent and child. For this reason I do not consider a three-way clash here.

I will now show that the child's interests have a certain priority, though not absolute priority, over another type of interest thought to be relevant to such decisions: the interest of potential parents in rearing their children.

Rejecting the Best Custodian Condition

In rejecting the best custodian condition Matthew Clayton argues that it places unacceptable opportunity costs on us as adults.[11] Adults who do not happen to be the best custodians are not permitted to rear the children they beget. This is a high price indeed since adults often derive a good deal of well-being from raising their children. The costs to adults of being denied custody of children over whom they have custody are high. This is so whether they are birth parents or adoptive parents. Now, one may think that the interest in being a parent is equally weighty whether you have a child or not, and it is true that many parents cannot conceive and this often leaves them childless when they would have made excellent parents. However, it seems sensible to say that having a child removed from your custody is, in many ways, far worse than being unable to conceive in the first place.[12] The situation of the parent who had the right to rear and has it removed is not analogous to the situation of the parent who is never given the right to rear and has their ambition to become a parent frustrated. There is a possible disanalogy between such parents with respect to the costs and attachments already present prior to the denial of custody. The interest a parent has in retaining the right to rear could well be weightier than the interest a parent has in initially acquiring the right to rear. This may affect the nature, and weight, of the values that clash.[13]

Under the best custodian condition some adults can have the right to rear removed, with high costs to themselves, even when they are good or even excellent parents, because there are other willing parents who would be much better. This is because under the best custodian condition it is not enough that someone would make a good or even an excellent parent. They must be better than all others in respect of the child's interests.

Clayton argues that while the child's interests are important, the best custodian condition gives too much priority to them.[14] With this I agree. He suggests that the truth of this claim becomes clear when we see the conflict as intra-personal and not inter-personal, that is, as a conflict within a person as a child and as an adult and not as a conflict between some child and some adult.

Thus, he concludes, it is sensible to trade off the child's interests for the adult's interests.

As children we have an interest in the quality of our upbringing being as good as possible. As adults we have an interest in pursuing our conception of the good and an important part of this for many is the opportunity to become a custodial parent and retain the right to rear. I will argue that the best custodian condition will make the wrong decision in a number of cases where, as a child, we are provided with at least a good enough upbringing, but as adults we lose the custody of our children. These examples suggest that some of the child's interests can be sacrificed for the sake of the adult's interest in retaining the right to rear. Given that we also think that there are some costs that cannot be imposed on children for the sake of their parents' interests, including neglect and abuse, this raises the problem of specifying how far the child's interests can usually be sacrificed for the adult's interests.

As children Ben and Yola received different upbringings in different societies. Ben lived under institutions governed by the best custodian condition. Yola lived under institutions governed by a threshold principle that insists that to retain the right to rear one must be good enough but that one need not be the best possible parent. As a result of the different upbringings they received, Ben's interests as a child were satisfied to a far greater degree than Yola's. Ben had a fantastic upbringing filled with love and care as well as with challenging opportunities, trips abroad, the greatest attention and educational toys. Yola did not receive many of these things but did receive love and attention, as well as decent toys and some opportunities.

As adults Ben and Yola wish to be parents. It is very important to their conception of the good that they retain the right to rear a child. Ben is a good parent. Ben has always cared very much about, and has always had the ambition of, rearing a child. Ben does not pose what we might think of as a serious harm to any child in his custody. Despite his aptitude as a custodial parent, Ben has his child removed from his custody because there is a better candidate parent available in his society. As a result Ben's life goes worse because of it.

Yola has similar qualities and ambitions to Ben. She has always wanted to be a parent and will make a good one. Since Yola's society is designed in accordance with a threshold conception of justice in the distribution of the right to rear, Yola needs only to meet the threshold to retain the right to rear over the children she begets. Yola will not satisfy the child's interests to a greater extent than Ben would have. Furthermore, many in Yola's society would make better parents than her. Nevertheless, Yola meets the threshold and will provide the child with at least as good an upbringing as her parents gave her and therefore retains the right to rear.

The question from this example is 'How do you think these people would choose to trade off their interests as adults and their interests as children?' I claim that both would prefer to have lived in the society with the threshold conception rather than the best custodian condition and that this preference is evidence of the threshold view being a highly plausible view of the demands of justice in this area. The example illustrates that it is reasonable to sacrifice some child's interests for some adult's interests. The reason for this is that Ben and Yola themselves would trade off their interests as children to meet their interests as adults.

However, Clayton's argument and the foregoing example have merely shown that we can sacrifice some of our interests as children for our interests as adults. Some might object to this as it is an inter-personal example and actual cases are inter-personal, involving a clash between the interests of two distinct persons. It is plausible to think that our willingness to make sacrifices in our own lives does not license us to make similar sacrifices involving the lives of others. For example, I might happily agree to invest a significant sum in a high-risk, high-reward venture but I cannot invest a similar sum of yours in that same venture because it seems rational to me. For this reason, it would be better if we had an inter-personal argument as well.

Now consider a realistic, but nonetheless stylised, pair of cases. Imagine that a certain way of feeding young children is better for their prospects than alternative methods of feeding and that it is very painful and difficult for many parents to feed in this way. In society A, which follows the best custodian view, parents who refuse to feed their children in this way, or are incapable of developing 'the knack', lose custody of their children just in case others are able and willing to feed those children in that way, and are equally good in other respects. Assume, also, that we have in mind children who are very young and as such are much less sensitive to the costs of instability and transition discussed above. In society B, the best custodian view is not followed and those parents are permitted to keep their children. One reason to prefer society B and reject the best custodian view would be that the benefits to the child are fairly small but the cost to the parent of losing custody is huge. At this stage, however, we do well to note that this is just one explanation of the conviction that society B is to be preferred and the best custodian view rejected.

It seems implausible to think that the child's interests always win the day. This gives us strong reasons to think that children should not always be removed from their parents simply because, under the custody of other parents, they would receive a superior upbringing, even in net terms. We must take into account the adult's interests too. If we want to answer important questions of policy, and guide and assess the design of institutional arrangements around child protection, we need to have a clearer idea of which of the child's interests are able to defeat the interest the adult has in retaining custody of their children. Moreover, in order to complete the dual interest view, we need to articulate and defend a particular threshold, the content of which will be given by the most important of the child's interests. Such interests will be those that, if violated, would usually be sufficient to deny someone the right to rear. It is not just the case that the dual interest view is the most plausible view but requires completion. Its completion is required for it to be considered the most plausible. If no plausible threshold can be defended, then it cannot guide policy and we cannot even assess its plausibility. All that has been shown so far is that the dual interest view has promise, but for this to support optimism about the prospects for sufficientarianism we must show that some specified dual interest view is relatively more plausible than its rivals and, additionally, that the threshold should have an extensive role in our thought about important practical debates. However, before that I want to consider another child-centred view that it may be thought could respond better to the problems with the best custodian view and capture the motivation behind the dual interest view.

The Satiable View

One response to the defects with the best custodian view is to hold a threshold view. On such views, so long as a parent does a good enough job, in terms of the child's interests, they are not usually liable to have their custodial rights removed. Another response, however, is more simplistic. I call this the 'satiable view' and it holds that only (some of) the child's interests matter, but that the relevant interests are satiable. As such, any parent who satisfies these interests is good enough and cannot lose custody even if someone else would do a better job. On this view, there is no value clash, it is just that not all of the child's interests matter.

First of all it is worth explaining why this view does not fall to the objections that the best custodian view does. Recall that the Plato Worry concerns denying good parents the right to rear their children where others can do a better job in terms of the child's interests. On this view, the child has only an entitlement to a good enough upbringing and not the best and so further improvements cannot count as reasons to redistribute child-rearing rights. So, in an example involving Good Parents and Best Parents, where Best Parents do better with respect to the child's interests, but Good Parents satisfy the central and satiable interests, we cannot prefer Best Parents and so do not face the Plato Worry. A further attractive feature of the view is its simplicity. It appeals only to one set of interests and this may partly be explained by Vallentyne's argument that a person cannot have rights over another person unless is it in the interests of the weaker party.[15] This vulnerability acts as an exclusionary reason, blocking non-child-centred reasons from being relevant. A further point to note is that the satiable view may seem to capture what motivated the dual interest view: that the costs to parents could be too high if they are denied the right to rear even when doing a good job. But on the satiable view there are no good reasons to deny parents the right to rear if they do a good job in terms of the satiable interests. For this reason, the sacrifice to parents is avoided, though not by design, only as a side-effect, since this view does not give direct significance to those interests. This is not an unattractive view, for these reasons. The satiable view, however, raises a few further questions that it cannot answer plausibly.[16]

Although parsimonious and simplistic, the satiable view is far from being unproblematic. Indeed, it is partly due to its simplicity that several difficult questions arise. One question raised by the satiable view is 'Why is it that the child's relevant interests are satiable rather than insatiable?' It is in attempting to answer this question that proponents of the satiable view become unstuck. They must insist either that children have interests only in a minimally decent upbringing, or else that they have interests in a high-quality upbringing. The lower they set the level of the good enough upbringing, the more implausible it looks to deny that children have an interest in further improvements. Children's lives can go better in important ways beyond having a minimally decent upbringing where their needs are met and their moral powers are somewhat cultivated. The higher they set the level of the good enough upbringing, the less able they are to resist the Plato Worry. This is because the higher the threshold of their interests, the more likely it is that intuitively good parents can lose out to better parents. Although this view does better than the best custodian view with respect to the Plato Worry, it is still not a completely satisfying response.

If there were no better explanation of the Plato Worry, then it would seem that we should accept the satiable view, but we should not. An alternative does exist that can avoid these worries. It also helps explain what is problematic about the Plato Worry without appeal to some intuitive notion of the good enough upbringing and thus coming close to begging the question. It also explains a further problem with the satiable view.

Before we consider how else to explain the Plato Worry, we should consider some more serious problems, the first of which is that the satiable view cannot explain what is lost where children are reared in institutions rather than by parents. According to the satiable view, if institutions rather than parents will meet the child's satiable interests, then we have no reason to prefer one or the other. But this view overlooks one important set of interests: those of the parent. One reason why we should favour parenting rather than equally good institutions is that it is good for parents to parent and, when they are denied this opportunity, they have their interests in pursuing a definite and valuable plan of life set back.

The Plato Worry can be explained by our concern for parents rather than a lack of concern for children after some point. Precisely what is worrying is that we think that good parents will lose custody and since they value child-rearing, their interests are seriously set back. Taking into account the parental interest, therefore, explains why it is that we need not only care about the child's interests. For these reasons we should favour a dual interest approach to the distribution of child-rearing rights and the conditions under which custody can be changed should be determined by considering both the interests of the child and those of the parent. On the dual interest approach, a value clash is possible and therefore a sufficientarian solution to it is possibly the most plausible way of dealing with it.

I propose that we see the parental interest in *retaining* custody over the child acting as a reason to refrain from securing the best upbringing for the child where that can only be achieved by denying the current parent custody. I see the parental interest and some of the child's interests as being defeasible and the parental interest can countervail some of the child's interests. In the next section I explain and defend this view in more detail before fleshing it out, but first a few clarificatory remarks about that approach are required.

The Value Clash Line of Argument

The value clash line of argument sees two interests as having some defeasible weight in determining what a good enough parent is. These are the interests of the parents in retaining custody and the interests of the child in having a better upbringing. Where some parents have custody over a child but by rearranging custody the interests of the child could be promoted, these interests do conflict. Note that this value clash does not occur where the child is not currently being reared by parents but is instead reared in some institutional setting, such as a group home. In such cases the best custodian is likely to be preferred since we only have the child's interests to be concerned with. Moreover, the satiable view, insofar as it is distinct from the best custodian view, could deny children a better upbringing if a worse upbringing was still good enough.

The value clash line of argument sees the interests of parents and children as capable of clashing in principle. Giving absolute priority to the interests of parents over the child is going to violate even the child's strongest interests, which is clearly unacceptable. Giving priority to the interests of the child is going to suffer from the same problems as the best custodian condition, albeit with some reference to parental interests in tie-break situations. A better response is to give priority to the child's interests up to a point and then to accept that the parental interests have greater weight. A good way of making sense of this idea is to see the child's interests as being of diminishing importance but the parental interest in retaining custody as remaining roughly the same regardless of how well the child's interests are promoted. In cases where the parent would do a very bad job we might suppose they do not have any weighty interest in retaining custody, but they do have such an interest over a wide range of cases. With the interests understood in this way, we can say that while the child's interests diminish in priority as their upbringing quality improves, initially outweighing the parental interests, they will eventually diminish such that the parental interest has greater weight. This is the basic idea behind the value clash line of argument and it supports the existence of a threshold at the point of the intersection. In the next section I will say more about how to specify the dual interest threshold and what the most plausible content of that threshold is likely to be.

An Account of a Good Enough Upbringing

When attempting to devise a suitable threshold of the good enough upbringing, two questions present themselves immediately:

1. How do we give content to an account of a good enough upbringing?
2. How do we work out whether one account is more plausible than another?

The first question draws our attention to the formal constraints that apply to any threshold and those that apply to a good enough upbringing threshold in particular. The answer to the first question will point us towards the kinds of content that can and cannot be given to the threshold. This will narrow down our search somewhat, but may leave us with a number of distinctive thresholds to choose from. Answers to the second question help us to decide between these thresholds and defend one threshold as the most plausible. I shall now answer each question in turn within the dual interest framework adopted through argument in the previous sections.

How do we fill out an account of a good enough upbringing? Some pertinent constraints of sufficiency thresholds have been identified in the opening chapters of the thesis and I shall repeat them here. Clearly, this particular threshold must focus only on the child's interests. This is a pertinent constraint because we are trying to distinguish between those of the child's interests that are especially important, and are therefore able to outweigh the adult's interest in retaining the right to rear, and those interests that can be more easily countervailed. An account of the good enough upbringing which included the interests of the parents would be odd indeed as it could lead to parents who do a good job by their children but sacrifice their own interests losing their right to rear, or to parents who do not do a particularly good job in terms of their child's interests but satisfy their own interests being considered good enough. Therefore, our first constraint is *child-centredness*.

Second, the content of any threshold must be satiable. This means that the threshold must be capable of being completely met, and once met it cannot and could not be met to a higher degree.[17] If the content given to the threshold is insatiable, then no one could be a good enough parent and therefore we would not have a suitable threshold that could resolve a conflict between two values. The child's interests would always win out if the child-centred threshold is insatiable and this would deny the value conflict. So we have a second constraint: *satiability*.

The content of a threshold must also be non-instrumental. If a child has an interest in being reared by his or her biological parents only because they are likely to be the best, then we should not include his or her interest in being reared by his or her biological parents among the interests relevant to decisions about the allocation of the right to rear. Instead, we should refer directly to the interest he or she has in being reared by the best parent. However, if a child has an interest in being reared by his or her biological parents because there is something non-instrumentally significant about being reared by those with whom we share genetic data or the process of gestation, then this may count as a non-instrumental reason, since it is a reasonably fixed part of our more fundamental interest.[18]

One further constraint on the content of this threshold is the *coincidence condition*. The coincidence condition requires that collectively the content of any adequate threshold is capable of accounting for our strongest intuitive judgements. For instance, a threshold that permitted abusive parents to be considered good enough would clearly be implausible. Also, a threshold that did not classify very good parents as good enough would be implausible. If a threshold does not, at least, account for our strong intuitive judgements, then the threshold cannot be plausible.

As I have said, we may find that the constraints do not leave us with one unique set of content for our threshold. There may be a number of possible thresholds that meet these constraints. I recommend that we decide between them, and therefore answer the second question, by testing the remaining thresholds by examining their plausibility where they are most likely to generate the most distinctive judgements. Thresholds are distinguished from one another by how low or high they are set, and the most counter-intuitive counter-examples will be found by appealing to cases involving the worst parent that qualifies as being good enough on that view.

We could rank the thresholds that meet the constraints in accordance with our intuitive reaction to their answer to this question, hoping that there will be a clear victor. However, we can and should attempt to be more systematic than this. From viewing the situation as a clash of value, we can see that it was the excessive opportunity costs to the adult that drew attention to the need for a threshold in the first place. Since the adult's interests are at stake, we must insist that the child's satiable interests, included in the threshold, are weightier than the adult's interest in advancing their conception of the good in the way that parenting does. If the content given to the threshold does not outweigh the adult's interest, then the threshold will impose excessive opportunity costs on adults. But in order to use this desideratum we need to try to get some idea of the weight of the adult's interest in retaining custody of his or her child.

Adults have an interest in *retaining* custody of their children that derives from an interest in advancing their conception of the good.[19] Denying some parent custody of his or her child frustrates that pursuit. It is argued that the relationship between a parent and a child makes a unique contribution to well-being that is not readily substituted by other relationships or combinations of relationships.[20] Summarising the literature, we can say that the relationship between a parent and child differs from relationships between adults. No adult–adult relationships, however intimate, are quite like parent–child relationships. Parent–child relationships are intimate relationships of unequal standing, the child, at least when young, has no resources to exit the relationship, unconditional and spontaneous love is often present, enjoyment and pleasure can be derived from observing the innocence and naivety of the child and his or her experiences, and the parent is charged with the responsibility of protecting the child when most vulnerable. Relationships between adults may share some of these qualities but no such relationships possess all these qualities. Relationships between two adults may sometimes proceed on an unequal footing, and it is clear that some adult partners may find it much more costly to exit marital relations. However, even in those cases weaker parties have a greater power of exit than young children do. It is a fact about adult–child relationships, at least when the child is young, that the child has no resources to exit.

The most analogous relationship is that of an adult and his or her mentally or physically deteriorating parent. Such a relationship may be one that proceeds on an unequal footing, and the parent cannot easily exit, but the ailing parent is not in the process of developing like a child is. A parent may take pride in seeing his or her child grow up and develop over time. He or she will not see an ailing parent develop over time. Usually the ailing parent is in decline and there is very little that can be done to slow that down. As such, it may be right for this adult child to take pride in having looked after the ailing parent but it is not the same kind of relationship and does not confer the same kinds of goods. It is not a relationship we aspire to enter into if the condition of the parent can be avoided, but the circumstances of the child are not like that. Moreover, these relationships are disanalogous in another respect. The ailing parent, being cared for by the adult child, could have made arrangements for what will happen if he or she declines, but the child cannot make plans for his or her vulnerability prior to being vulnerable.

The parent–child relationship presents various challenges for parents that are not posed by other intimate relationships, such as the relationships between two lovers or friends. Overcoming these challenges and succeeding in encouraging a child's development from a unique caring position makes a profound contribution to the success of one's life as a whole. Being denied such relationships, when one is established, imposes significant costs on an adult in terms of his or her well-being. He or she is denied this setting in which to pursue the goods he or she prizes. So what is the best way of characterising this interest generally so that we might understand the weight of the loss to the parent that will be important in assessing whether any threshold imposes excessive opportunity costs on parents?

Matthew Clayton describes the interest as a member of the kind of interest we have 'in maintaining intimate relationships with particular dependent others', an interest we all may have, even those of us who do not want children.[21] However, characterising the interest in this way does not recognise the uniqueness of the parent–child relationship and suggests a weaker weight than what Brighouse and Swift identify as a relationship that contributes 'to well-being in a quite distinctive way'.[22] It cannot be easily substituted, on their view, and as such should be given a special kind of priority. In light of the foregoing discussion, and drawing on both of these views, I believe that we should characterise the relationship as one that makes a distinctive and weighty contribution to well-being. Characterising the interest in this way will allow us to attach a certain weight to it relative to the kinds of interests a child has in his or her well-being and thus will make setting the good enough level of upbringing more tractable.

To recap, then, we are looking to give content to the threshold by appeal to satiable, child-centred interests and the combination of such interests must be capable of explaining our strongest relevant intuitive judgements. We rank possible thresholds that meet all of these constraints in terms of the plausibility of their answers to the question 'How bad can a good enough parent be?' To do so we test whether each interest is weightier than the adult's interest in retaining the right to rear that makes a distinctive and weighty contribution to his or her well-being. This is the value clash line of argument for sufficientarian principles and it will help us give content to the threshold from which we can derive judgements about practical issues.

The Thresholds

Having laid out the criteria with respect to which we are to assess accounts of the good enough upbringing, there are two possible ways to proceed. One way to proceed would be to assess particular interests that are putatively important against the criteria set out above. Another way to proceed would be to divide the child's interests in flourishing into various general categories and to assess various combinations of those categories as content for a threshold using the criteria set out above. First, I consider two putatively important child's interests: the two moral powers, and love. I then dismiss these as being sufficient for a threshold and dismiss this kind of approach, though I draw some important insights from it. Second, I opt for an approach that identifies general kinds of interests in flourishing as ones that can complete the most plausible threshold since it is an adult's interest in flourishing with which they must successfully clash. I conclude that a good enough parent is one who will promote the child's independence and will provide the child with the essential conditions for leading a good life and the unique goods of childhood. A good enough parent can fall short in some important areas, namely, with respect to the child's interests that can be advanced in adulthood and with respect to some conditions that are merely conducive to living a good life. This, I will argue, provides us with the most satisfactory answer to the question 'How bad can a good enough parent be?' of the candidate thresholds, and thus provides us with a further relatively indispensable sufficientarian principle.

All You Need is Love

Some theorists have discussed unconditional love as an important part of a good upbringing.[23] Some even go so far as to say that children have a right to be loved.[24] Liao argues that a child's right to love comes from a more general right all human beings have to those conditions that are essential for a good life.[25] To be suited to our threshold love must satisfy the aforementioned constraints. To see whether it does so we need to understand what is meant by love. Liao claims that parental love can be explained in the following way:

> To love a child is to seek a highly intense interaction with the child, where one values the child for the child's sake, where one seeks to bring about and to maintain physical and psychological proximity with the child, where one seeks to promote the child's well-being for the child's sake, and where one desires that the child reciprocate or, at least, is responsive to one's love.[26]

Liao's definition of love, at least with respect to the love one has for one's children, does not seem eccentric. It captures what we mean by love as something that can be of value to the child and sees love as child-centred. Furthermore, love, so understood, is satiable. It seems that a parent can meet this requirement and love his or her child in this sense. One can seek to promote the child's well-being and one can value the child for his or her own sake. So this interest is child-centred, and satiable.

With respect to the final constraint, the coincidence condition, we can say that it seems that the parents who are obviously good enough do seem to love their children, and that some bad parents do not love their children. However, love does not seem to be what is at stake in cases of abuse. All one has to do to love the child in Liao's sense is to *seek* a certain kind of relationship with the child. A parent can, however, have good intentions, and yet still be a bad parent. Here we might find it helpful to distinguish between the *evil* and the *incompetent* parent.

The evil parent intends to harm the child, perhaps for his or her own pleasure. Such a parent has no intention of seeking the kind of relationship that Liao describes. Clearly, the evil parent is not a good enough parent, but the evil parent does not meet the love threshold. The example of the evil parent, then, is a test passed by the love threshold. However, the same cannot be said of the incompetent parent. The incompetent parent loves the child in the sense Liao articulates. However, the incompetent parent leaves the very young child in hot cars and on park benches on sunny days and fails to feed him or her properly, thinking, say, that yeast extract contains all the nutrition a growing child needs. The incompetent parent does meet the love threshold but is clearly not a good enough parent. As such, the love threshold cannot be the correct threshold. Love is not all you need to be a good enough parent.

Having objected to the term 'seek', we might revise the account given by Liao and replace 'seek' with 'achieve'. After all, it is more clearly in the child's interests that the valuable relationship is achieved than it is to claim that the child has a right to someone seeking a highly intense relationship with him or her. However, before going further it is worthwhile considering why Liao's focus is on seeking and not on achieving. This is because Liao is interested in establishing a right to love, which must have a corresponding duty and, since it is not in the power of the will of anyone to achieve love of any particular child, it is difficult to argue that children have a right to be loved because it is difficult to argue that adults have a duty to love, in fact. But a similar worry does not arise for me, since I am not concerned with establishing that children have a right to love, but rather that they have an interest in it and, given its importance, it seems that it could count as ground for denying someone custody if they would not love the child in question.

In order to evaluate the notion of achieving love as a weighty interest of the child, we would need to examine more closely what is involved in a loving relationship. The way set out by Liao is too imprecise. There may be enormous instrumental benefits to having a custodial parent who loves you, who is willing to make sacrifices that others would not, and loving relationships might be good candidates for being intrinsically valuable too, but we think that such relationships are valuable because we have an ideal of such a relationship in mind, with particular qualities and interests protected. The qualities we are likely to state when listing what constitutes a loving relationship are likely to reflect our own experiences and to lack the generality required for our discussion. We need some greater reflective distance from the issue than the notion of love can provide if we are to articulate some very important general interests of children that would be suitable for a principle of justice. I will now move on to consider the putatively important moral powers.

Two Moral Powers

John Rawls held that when assessing competing accounts of the demands of justice, two interests are of paramount importance. These are: (1) the development of a capacity for a conception of the good, which is a capacity to revise, refine and rationally pursue a conception of the good life, and (2) a sense of justice, which is a motivation to comply with and the ability to understand the demands of justice.[27] I will now argue that these interests alone do not provide us with an acceptable threshold since they cannot meet the coincidence condition.

As these two interests are specified in Rawls they are satiable, so it seems that a parent could aim to fully satisfy these interests and in so doing be a good enough parent on this view. Rawls considers these interests to be fundamental and so they are also non-instrumental as is required for our threshold. Moreover, they are interests the child has and so they would be able to constitute a threshold that was child-centred.

The interest we have in the two moral powers, however, does not meet the coincidence condition. Some violations of the good enough upbringing will be linked to falling short with respect to the two moral powers. Consider the following example of abuse that threatens both moral powers. An upbringing that denied a person development of his or her capacities for rational planning and inculcated unreasonable views and motivations regarding the treatment of those who believe differently to him- or herself would be unacceptable. Those brought up as child soldiers, for example, have not had a good enough upbringing. The custodial arrangements of such a child ought to be changed. So it seems that these kinds of examples can be correctly identified by a Rawls-inspired threshold.

However, these interests fail the second part of the coincidence condition. The two moral powers can explain some violations of a good enough upbringing, but they cannot explain other important violations. The two moral powers do not, for example, seem to be what is at stake in many cases of child abuse or neglect. A sense of justice and a capacity for a conception of the good may not be set back by an abusive childhood and yet we would strongly consider abusive parents to have been not good enough to the extent that we would surely prefer the best custodian condition to apply, notwithstanding the excessive opportunity costs for adults.

A further difficulty with the Rawls-inspired threshold is that these interests focus on the child as if the only interests he or she has are *developmental*, that is, these interests derive their importance wholly from future benefits that will accrue in adulthood. Developmental accounts of a child's interests would focus solely on preparing the child for a good adulthood at the expense of any of the special goods of childhood. It seems that there are especially important non-developmental interests a child has in having a good upbringing that should not be sacrificed.[28] Consider the following example. Imagine there is a pill that enables you to by-pass your good enough childhood and you take it. Whatever else we thought about your decision, we would think that your life was lacking in some important sense because you never had access to the goods, the experiences and the relationships that are only available to you when you are a child. It is held by some that there are important goods unique to childhood, perhaps associated with the innocence that we can never regain.[29] Such goods are time-sensitive. It is true that some time-sensitive goods are developmental, but not all are. Even rejecting the example, and thinking that we have sufficient reason to take the pill, one might think that our time as a child can be better spent with respect to goods available only in childhood that are not developmental. It seems, then, that this threshold is inadequate because it fails to meet the coincidence condition and fails to adequately account for some goods distinctively available in childhood that seem to have a certain importance. When specifying the threshold, then, we should be aware of the goods available to children that are non-developmental.

A More General Approach

In the preceding sections I have explored one method of filling out the content of the threshold that appealed to some specific interests a child has that have been regarded as being especially important. However, looking at specific interests has been unsatisfying. I believe we do better to focus on a more general specification of the interests that can fill out the content of a threshold. This allows us greater reflective distance and the opportunity to find a principled distinction between the kinds of interests that should be regarded as especially important, and hence part of the threshold. This should reassure us that we are not just picking our favourite parts of our own childhood and that we are collecting together the types of interests that it seems plausible to claim are especially important.[30]

In this section I will distinguish between the relevant sets of interests children have that can be both developmental and non-developmental. I will then argue that some sets seem relatively more important than the adult's interest in retaining the right to rear and argue that these sets of interests should give content to the threshold. One concern about this particular strategy is that it is too abstract to provide guidance but I will show that it does help us make some decisions, though it is limited in what it can do, and it also achieves an important philosophical task of focussing our attention on what sorts of more concrete claims can be advanced within this framework. As such, the general approach helps narrow our focus and makes this highly difficult problem more tractable.

The child's interests in a good life can be divided up into different categories, some of which are non-developmental. A sensible way of proceeding would be to see weight or special importance as attaching to interests in virtue of their category and each category being given weight in accordance with their centrality to human flourishing. In addition this helps us to achieve the reflective distance required to cut through the prejudice that underlies some intuitions on this emotive topic. I focus on the child's interests in a good life and the categories of those interests as this will help us to judge their weight relative to the adult's interest that is at stake: the interest in retaining the right to rear. This framework should help us to assess the relative weight of the clashing interests in this case.

A child has an interest in pursuing a good life and from this we can infer that a child has an interest in those conditions conducive to living a good life. We can break down the category of conditions conducive to living a good life into five sub-categories:

1. Children have an interest in the conditions essential for a good life.
2. Children have an interest in the conditions conducive to a good life that are uniquely available in childhood.
3. Children have an interest in becoming independent and therefore being able to realise the conditions conducive to a good life available only in adulthood.
4. Children have an interest in the conditions conducive to a good life available in both adulthood and childhood.
5. Children have an interest in all other conditions conducive to a good life which are not covered by the above categories.

This categorisation exhausts the child's interests in a good life. I will argue that the combination of interests 1–3 provides us with the most plausible account of a good enough upbringing. I take each set of interests in order and show that 1–3 are each necessary and in combination sufficient for a good enough upbringing. I then dismiss a more demanding threshold involving 4 and then 5.

Essential Conditions for a Good Life

Recall that Liao argues that a child has a right to love because that child has a right to the conditions essential for a good life. The set of '*conditions essential for a good life*' make up a set of child's interests and one set that we might think is a very good candidate for the special importance required to be part of our threshold. The conditions essential for a good life are child-centred since the child has an interest in them. Furthermore, they are satiable. This can be illustrated by the fact that people do live good lives, though some lives are better than others.

Clearly the child has an interest in living a good life and so has an interest in those conditions essential for a good life. It seems that we should attach a special priority to those conditions essential for a good life. Any parent unable to provide such conditions would surely not be good enough and would therefore usually lose their immunity to being denied custody. This can be further illustrated by considering the weight requirement. The conditions essential for a good life are more important than what is at stake for the potential parents: a distinctive and weighty part of their well-being. Retaining the right to rear is not a necessary condition of living a good life and so it has a lesser priority than those necessary conditions. While the parent who is denied the right to rear can live a good life, the person who was denied a good enough upbringing because he or she was denied the conditions essential for a good life cannot. The costs to the person of an inadequate childhood far outweigh the costs to the adult denied the right to rear.

The conditions required for a good life outweigh those conditions conducive to a good life and those goods that make a distinctive and weighty contribution to well-being. They meet the weight requirement since the conditions essential for a good life are more important than the adult's interest in being a parent, which is not essential for him or her to live a good life. Since it passes the weight requirement, it is a necessary part of the threshold.

However, it seems implausible to think that the conditions essential for a good life alone constitute a good enough upbringing. It seems that even when these conditions are secured, sacrifices in terms of the interests of the child can be sufficient for removing the right to rear. Consider whether the coincidence condition is met for such a threshold. Many people live good lives having been abused or neglected in their childhood so the paradigm examples of bad parents would not be ruled out by this threshold. This threshold would also not rule out amputating the child's leg or arm, or intentionally blinding the child, since limbs or sight are not essential for a good life. So, we must look to add to our threshold.

Goods Available Uniquely in Childhood

In discussing issues surrounding children and the family, Harry Brighouse and Adam Swift pick out a class of goods conducive to a good life: the goods distinctively available through the family.[31] Here I will focus on a similar but distinct category since I want to leave open the possibility that institutions can provide a good enough upbringing. Brighouse and Swift appeal to these familial relationship goods when justifying the institution of the family rather than other child-rearing institutions. I need make no such claim and can instead focus on a broader but similar category of goods: those goods conducive to a good life and uniquely available in childhood.

The goods available uniquely in childhood will include some of the goods that Brighouse and Swift identify as justifying family life since some of these goods are child-centred. These include loving attention, a sense of belonging, and the security of having a particular other care for your well-being when vulnerable. But our category is wider and will also include other goods that are available only in childhood but not exclusively in the family.[32] Some such goods might be available in the family and in child-rearing institutions, but not available once we become adults. As such, these goods are time-sensitive.

The goods that are available only in childhood seem more urgent, for the purposes of a good enough upbringing, than other goods that are conducive to a good life and other goods available in adulthood. Children can acquire the other goods later upon acquiring their independence and so their realisation lacks the same urgency and therefore weight for determining a good enough upbringing. As such, it makes more sense to insist that parents have responsibility for these and that responsibility for the other goods can be more widely distributed. Therefore, the lives of those who miss out on goods that are available to them when they become independent adults are not set back by their childhood to the same degree as they would have been had they missed out on goods unique to childhood.

Understanding this in a different way, we can see that it is imperative that parents give greater weight to securing those goods for the child than those that can be obtained by the child once he or she becomes an adult. These goods pass the weight requirement since they seem to be more important than the contribution being a parent makes to one's well-being. Indeed, an adult can reapply for the right to rear at a later date or else make provision for improving the quality of the upbringing he or she could offer a child. But a child who misses out on the goods unique to childhood cannot rerun his or her childhood. I suggest, then, that we add the goods unique to childhood to our threshold so that it includes both the conditions essential to a good life and the goods uniquely available in childhood as they both seem to have a special priority over other goods conducive to a good life.

Taking this section together with the previous section, we have an account that contains both the conditions essential for a good life and the goods uniquely available in childhood. Let us test this account by how it answers the question 'How bad can a good enough parent be?' It seems that more familiar sorts of abuse are ruled out by including the goods available only in childhood. Having a loving, secure and safe environment away from abuse must be part of the conditions conducive to a good life which are only available in childhood due to the unique vulnerability of the child. So this threshold seems less implausible than the previous one with respect to the coincidence condition, which permitted intentionally causing blindness and the removal of limbs, but there is still room for improvement.

One thing that is not mentioned in this (1–2) threshold is the idea of independence. The role of a custodial parent is sometimes thought to be justified only while the child develops independence.[33] Indeed, independence is required since without it those other goods, conducive to a good life in later life, could not be pursued. Independence is especially important and in order to meet the *coincidence condition*, it must be included.

We think that children can grow up too soon and that they can be held back from developing their independence. This interest is child-centred, it is satiable since some do become independent, and it meets the weight requirement for the following reasons. If a good enough parent can fail to develop a child's independence, then it seems that we would be dissatisfied with this threshold. This is partly because the child's interest in independence is weightier than the adult's interest in retaining the right to rear. Without independence one cannot enjoy a great many aspects of a good life. Moreover, without independence our justification for marking out the goods uniquely available in childhood as having priority over the goods obtainable in both adulthood and childhood no longer stands. Our next step, then, should be to see if we can add a concern for independence to the threshold in a way that does not jeopardise the progress we have already made with respect to the threshold.

Independence

Children have an interest in becoming independent and a good enough upbringing must be consistent with the development of their independence. What counts as independence will vary from society to society, and the rate at which one should develop independence varies from society to society but at a minimum it must contain the prerequisites for pursuing a variety of goods in adulthood since that formed part of the conditions that allowed us to give priority to the goods uniquely available in childhood. I draw this account of independence from the Rawlsian moral powers discussed above.

With the addition of independence the threshold seems to enable us to account for important interests of a child and to meet the coincidence condition because this blocks the independence objections to the good enough upbringing threshold and shows that this threshold is more plausible than the aforementioned thresholds. In the next section I will consider an intuitive comparison between this threshold and others and will argue that the account set out here is the most plausible account available since it answers the question 'How bad can a good enough parent be?' better than any other.

The Conditions Conducive to a Good Life

We could add to our threshold (1–3) the interests the child has in the conditions conducive to a good life (4–5) but I think this is a step too far. Children have an interest in the conditions most conducive to a good life. This includes the conditions essential for a good life, the goods available uniquely in childhood, and the goods available in both childhood and adulthood. This threshold would be distinguished from the previous threshold by the inclusion of the goods available in both childhood and adulthood that are conducive to a good life. But including these conditions in our threshold would effectively award the child's interests priority over the adult's in all cases and hence would dissolve the conflict of interests on which this problem is premised. This can be noted by observing that we identified all the child's interests as being exhausted by his or her interest in the conditions conducive to living a good life.

We can, however, take a step back. We could add to our (1–3) threshold only the goods available in both adulthood and childhood (4). This would avoid the problem of reducing the threshold to the best custodian condition as the addition of further conditions conducive to a good life would. However, this is still a step too far since the goods available in both adulthood and childhood lack the requisite importance to outweigh what is at stake for the adult: a distinctive and important part of a good life.

To illustrate this point consider two possible parents Carole and Xavier, both of whom want the right to rear and would provide the child with the conditions essential for a good life, the unique goods of childhood, and would promote the child's independence at a rate not inconsistent with common knowledge. However, Carole would provide the child with some of the goods that are available to both adults and children but Xavier would not. Let us imagine for example that Carole can provide the child with extensive piano tuition and driving lessons that Xavier would not, perhaps because Xavier thinks that learning the piano is a waste of a child's time and that in order to provide the child with driving lessons, Xavier would have to own private land but he does not own private land.

An adult can learn the piano and learn to drive without prior experience. Under Carole's care these experiences are conducive to a good life. Having an appreciation for the piano, mastering difficult skills, will contribute to the well-being of the child and the adult he or she becomes. Learning to drive earlier probably makes the child less likely to crash his or her car and be reckless with it, and it will save the child the cost and frustration of driving lessons later on in adulthood. But these seem like goods of our childhood that Xavier would willingly trade off, if he could, for the opportunity to retain custody of his child. Imagine that Xavier has custody of the child and Carole promises, in good faith, to give Xavier's child piano lessons and driving lessons if she can have custody of the child. I believe it is counter-intuitive to think that a good enough parent must be as good as Carole. I believe, then, that we should reject this threshold and prefer the threshold that includes only independence, conditions essential for a good life and the goods uniquely available in childhood because it better meets the weight requirement.

How Bad Can a Good Enough Parent Be?

I have said that a good enough parent, that is, one who cannot usually be denied the right to rear, will protect the especially important interests in the conditions essential for a good life and the goods uniquely available in childhood (1–2), alongside securing independence understood as the two moral powers (3). I must now say something about what these goods are in order to assess how bad a good enough parent can be on this view and to draw out its implications.

What are the conditions essential for a good life? Survival is required, of course, but securing these conditions does not really take us much further. This condition likely rules out reckless parents who leave their children in the temporary custody of wild or captive animals, hold their children over balconies or refuse their children life-saving blood transfusions.[34] But it does not seem to rule out amputating a child's leg or arm, or making the child blind since limbs and sight are not essential for a good life.

The upbringing of the child by a good enough parent must include those interests the child has that are weightier than an important part of a good life equivalent to the adult's interest in not being denied the right to rear. I have called this the 'weight requirement'. I have categorised children's interests and have shown that those conditions essential for a good life, and those goods made distinctively available in childhood, cannot be compromised. However, a set of interests that can be promoted in childhood but are nevertheless available later in life may be compromised by a good enough parent. So when designing policy, we must consider parents who are likely to fall short with respect to independence, the conditions essential for a good life, or with respect to the goods distinctively available in childhood, as not being good enough. However, those who fall short in other ways will not be considered not good enough and can usually retain custody of their children.

Good enough parents may send their children to an inferior school, not help them with their homework or not provide them with the most nutritious meals. Of course, a loving parent–child relationship will likely be a special good of childhood and it requires shared interests and so it is likely that some shared interests will be required, but not a large number of such interests.[35] These shortfalls for the child are no weightier than the adult's interest in being a parent, which is a distinctive and important part of a good life. Overall, then, this combination of children's interests seems the best. The shortfalls are significant, but they are not excessive. A good enough parent can be so bad that he or she fails to provide the child with the goods that he or she could acquire later on as an adult and this is the point where the value clash will generate a change in the importance of the child's interest relative to that of the adult.

Applications and Implications

Having identified and defended an account of a good enough upbringing, I will now consider the account's implications for redistribution. I will also evaluate actual policy guidelines regarding the allocation of the right to rear and will suggest some revisions to current policy on adoption, fostering and taking children into care. I claim that this account of the good enough upbringing should have an extensive role in our thought about practical debates.

Justice

One concern we have relevant to the good enough upbringing pertains to distributive justice and the resources required to become a good enough parent. It seems that while some adults will not want to be parents at all, others have a strong interest in being good enough because it is only then that they can usually retain custody of their children. This likely requires greater training and assistance for those who have this interest and we should consider this interest as having great weight. One implication of the account I have offered is that society be structured so as to be the kind of place in which children will receive a good enough upbringing. Of course, many factors other than who your parents are affect the quality of your upbringing along the dimensions I have discussed.

Parents bringing up their children in a neighbourhood with high infant mortality rates, high crime, low employment, poor schools and poor healthcare provision will find it much more difficult to meet the threshold than parents bringing up their children in areas with far better provision. This insufficiency calls for redress.

Where you happen to be brought up should not affect whether your upbringing was above or below the threshold. Adapting our society, redistributing resources and supporting parents whose ability to parent is negatively affected by their circumstances provide very important policy goals. This is perhaps the best way to ensure that a generation of children receive a good enough upbringing. It specifies conditions suitable for the upbringing of children.

Sometimes parents can do nothing about the fact that their children will not meet the threshold. Social problems blight the lives of children. The threshold sets a defensible level of well-being that a child must reach in a moderately just society. It is, in the spirit of sufficientarianism, especially important for children to secure a good enough upbringing. Thereafter, competing considerations can more easily outweigh this demand. It may prove very difficult to specify exactly how much weight to give this threshold relative to other demands of justice but it can be said that providing children with a good enough upbringing is an especially important part of justice. Therefore, we have weighty reasons to organise society such that every child's upbringing meets the good enough level, but our reasons to further improve the quality of their upbringing, beyond the threshold, are much less weighty. An implication of this shift may be that all members of society should share the costs of upbringing up to the good enough level, but that further improvements should be made at parents' discretion. Our reasons to promote the child's welfare beyond this point, I have argued, are more easily outweighed by other considerations and one such consideration may be the ambition sensitivity of the distribution of benefits and burdens. This sets a suitable threshold of state provision for parents. The overall cost of a good enough upbringing is to be shared. We may still have weighty reasons to support child-rearing through tax and transfer policy, perhaps to ensure greater distributive justice in other ways, or perhaps to promote the general welfare, but these reasons will not be as strong as our reasons to ensure that children receive a good enough upbringing.[36]

Furthermore, the good enough parent threshold also provides us with a principle for designing child-rearing institutions. We have seen that it is especially important that any child's interests in the conditions essential for a good life, and for the goods uniquely available in childhood, are given special priority over other less central goods. It may be argued that some of the goods that are uniquely available in childhood are not available in institutions. A candidate for such a good is the good of having a loving and intimate relationship with a particular other charged with promoting the child's well-being, such as a parent.[37] I am not sure what I think of the veracity of this claim, but it is clear that the standard can be used to assess the design of institutions of this sort. If some goods included within the threshold cannot be obtained in institutions, then we cannot insist it be realised, but this gives us an important reason to prefer the best possible parents over the best possible institutions.

In light of this discussion, it seems that the principle of a good enough upbringing provides us with an important standard of distributive justice and provides us with important guidance with respect to certain policy areas. This bodes well for the prospects of sufficientarianism.

Policy

In this section I will use the threshold I have articulated to evaluate current policy in the UK regarding child custody. I will first of all explain some background to the policy then discuss the criteria currently used to decide on whether to deny parents custody of their children.

In 1989 the Children Act was introduced in the UK. The Children Act utilised the concept of significant harm as the threshold that justifies compulsory intervention in family life. This concept of significant harm, we might think, suggests a suitable threshold perhaps mirroring the function of the account of a good enough upbringing that I have defended. We should note, however, that this threshold concerns the circumstances in which we *must* intervene, and not merely the circumstances in which we may usually intervene in a particular way, by denying parents custody of their children, as my threshold states. This is a subtle difference in the purpose of both standards, but we can assess the policy threshold in light of the account of the good enough upbringing I give since they both pass judgement on the grounds that are, at least, usually sufficient for denying parents custody of their children.

In a number of documents we are told that there are 'no absolute criteria on which to rely when judging what constitutes significant harm'.[38] Some rough guidelines are given to social workers from the council or government, and so I will comment on these:

> To understand and establish significant harm, it is necessary to consider:
> - the nature of harm, in terms of maltreatment or failure to provide adequate care
> - the impact on the child's health and development
> - the child's development within the context of their family and wider environment
> - any special needs, such as a medical condition, communication impairment or disability, that may affect the child's development and care within the family
> - the capacity of parents to meet adequately the child's needs
> - the wider and environmental family context.[39]

The notion of significant harm as used in these guidelines is not one that can easily be understood as stemming from a single abstract notion. These guidelines merely list the commonly experienced types of maltreatment of children. This makes the guidelines hard to critique individually since they are essentially statements of our considered convictions, but we can add to the list by identifying things that are not permitted by the threshold I have defended.

We might begin by adding to the list a more general demand that risks to the child's life are to be prohibited. Often these will take the form of health needs, but they also include other kinds of recklessness not mentioned in the list of factors above. Since living through childhood is usually essential for a good life, these kinds of treatment, which take important risks with the child's life, would seem to fit the kinds of significant harm we should focus on. Of course, it is important to note here that the case for holding a child over a balcony or allowing a child to explore a gorilla's cage can be made more satisfactorily than the case for denying a child a blood transfusion as the latter is always a large risk to the child's life. Having said that, we may hope that warnings, surveillance and targeted interventions can be used. Practitioners, though, should be alert to the fact that the threshold is likely to be breached.

Of course, in practice, we should also be aware and give due weight to existing injustices. Not all parents are given an equal or adequate opportunity to succeed at parenting. It is far more challenging for some parents to provide an adequate upbringing and this is undoubtedly a source of unfairness. For any case where a parent will fail to provide an adequate upbringing we can ask whether we ought to deny that parent custody or whether we should offer further support to him or her. In cases of background injustice, such as inadequate opportunities to be an adequate parent, the onus is likely to be strongly on the state and others to support the parent. These cases are particularly acute when members of particular cultural or ethnic groups are seriously and unjustly disadvantaged. If the adequate upbringing operates on its own, it could have the additional problematic consequence of particular cultural groups dying out. As such, the adequate upbringing must be taken against a background of other principles and judgements about when, all things considered, we may deny parents custody, which should be informed by those principles. But nevertheless, there is a value clash and it is one that sufficientarian principles are well placed to resolve plausibly.

Conclusion

In this chapter I have argued that there is a role for sufficiency when considering the way in which the right to rear should be distributed. In defence of the role for sufficiency in this debate I have defended a threshold conception against the best custodian conception of the distribution of the right to rear and I also gave particular content to that threshold. In giving content to the threshold I defended, and rendered more complete, dual interest accounts of the right to rear. I then drew out some important implications for policy from the threshold by focussing on the shortcomings of actual policy. This chapter completes a further task in the assessment of the prospects for sufficientarianism since it not only shows that one already prominent, but incomplete, role for sufficiency is sound, but it also shows how one can fill out that threshold and that the value clash line of argument can work. In doing so I have shown how one can fill out thresholds like this and how one can further defend this sufficiency view against important objections. I conclude that we should be optimistic about the prospects for sufficientarianism because there is a further indispensable sufficientarian principle that should have an extensive role in our thought about practical debates.

The next chapter addresses one of the most lively of recent debates in political philosophy: global justice. In that chapter I will further show that sufficientarian principles have much to offer and that the shift understanding of sufficientarianism has particular advantages over both sufficientarian and non-sufficientarian approaches to global justice.

Notes

1. This chapter is derived, in part, from Liam Shields, 'How bad can a good enough parent be?', *Canadian Journal of Philosophy*, 1–21, published online 18 February 2016, DOI: 10.1080/ 00455091.2016.1148306, available at <http://wwww.tandfonline. com/10.1080/00455091.2016.1148306> (last accessed 24 March 2016).
2. Brighouse and Swift, 'Legitimate parental partiality'.
3. Brighouse and Swift, 'Parents' rights and the value of the family'; Clayton, *Justice and Legitimacy in Upbringing*, 49; Gheaus, 'The right to parent one's biological baby'; Schoeman, 'Rights of children, rights of parents, and the moral basis of the family'; Vallentyne, 'The rights and duties of childrearing'.
4. Brighouse and Swift, 'Legitimate parental partiality', 52–3.
5 For discussion of how children have been viewed, including as property of their parents, see the Introduction to Archard and Macleod, *Moral and Political Status of Children*, 1–15.
6. 'BBC Profile: Josef Fritzl'.
7. Gheaus, 'The right to parent one's biological baby'.

8. In Vallentyne, 'The rights and duties of childrearing', 997, the author states: 'Second, possession of the childrearing rights by this person must be at least as good for the child (in terms of expected benefits) as possession by anyone else who both claims the rights and satisfies the no custodian condition. Call this the "best custodian condition". Together, these conditions hold that a person has childrearing rights over a child only if she claims them and it is in the (expected) best interests of the child for this person to have these childrearing rights, as compared to having no custodian or some other interested custodian for whom the no-custodian condition is satisfied.' Also see ibid., 998, where the author states: 'The claim is not that children have a right to be brought up by those who would give them the best upbringing. It is only that they have an immunity right not to be brought up by certain individuals when other willing individuals would do a better job for the child. Those for whom possession of childrearing rights would best promote the child's interests have the moral power to obtain those rights, but they generally do not have a duty to exercise that power and acquire the childrearing rights.'

9. This raises interesting questions about when and whether we can force people to care for children.

10. The idea of a child as a resource monster that I discuss here draws on Robert Nozick's discussion of a Utility-Monster in *Anarchy, State, Utopia*, 41–2.

11. Clayton, *Justice and Legitimacy in Upbringing*, 52–61.

12. Brighouse and Swift, *Family Values*.

13. Harry Brighouse and Adam Swift express this thought in their *Family Values*, 96.

14. Clayton, *Justice and Legitimacy in Upbringing*, 58.

15. Vallentyne, 'The rights and duties of childrearing'.

16. Hannan and Vernon, 'Parental rights: a role-based approach'.

17. Raz, *The Morality of Freedom*, 235.

18. For an example of an interest stemming from genetics, see Velleman, 'Family history'. For an example stemming from gestation, see Gheaus, 'The right to parent one's biological baby'.

19. It may be that the weight of an adult's interest in parenting varies in strength. If this is so, then the value clash I pick out will not always be the correct one. However, my claim is that the principle will get the right answer usually and this approach is more plausible than the rival ones. Moreover, we have reasons of simplicity to assume that the role of being a parent has roughly the same significance for all who have it. Without this assumption no general principle could

be devised and so we would have to resort to more or less ad hoc judgements that we could have no confidence in.

20. Brighouse and Swift, 'Parents' rights and the value of the family'; Clayton, *Justice and Legitimacy in Upbringing*; Schoeman, 'Rights of children, rights of parents, and the moral basis of the family'; Schrag, 'Justice and the family'.
21. Clayton, *Justice and Legitimacy in Upbringing*, 59.
22. Brighouse and Swift, 'Parents' rights and the value of the family', 96.
23. Brighouse and Swift, 'Legitimate parental partiality'; Hannan and Vernon, 'Parental rights: a role-based approach'; Liao, 'The right of children to be loved'; Schrag, 'Justice and the family'.
24. Liao, 'the right of children to be loved', 422.
25. Ibid., 422.
26. Ibid., 422.
27. Rawls, *Justice as Fairness*, 18–19.
28. Macleod, 'Primary goods, capabilities, and children'.
29. In Brighouse and Swift, 'Legitimate parental partiality', 53, the authors state: 'Here are some examples of relationship goods that can be realized or produced by the family: (1) Children enjoy the loving attention of, and bond with, a particular adult, a relationship that is widely regarded as essential for their emotional development. (2) Children enjoy a sense of continuity with (or belonging or attachment to) the past, mediated by acquaintance with their own family members. (3) Children enjoy the security provided by the presence of someone with a special duty of care for them.' For further discussion of intrinsic goods of childhood, see Brennan, 'The intrinsic goods of childhood'; Macleod, 'Primary goods, capabilities, and children'.
30. Instead of understanding what matters in terms of interests, we could understand what matters in terms of ambitions as Dworkin does in *Sovereign Virtue*. See Clayton, *Justice and Legitimacy in Upbringing* for a hybrid approach that takes into account interests and ambitions and deals with issues of justice in upbringing.
31. Brighouse and Swift, 'Legitimate parental partiality'.
32. Macleod, 'Primary goods, capabilities, and children', 187–9.
33. This is called the 'fiduciary' model of parenting and is discussed in Noggle, 'Special agents'.
34. 'TV star's baby handed to gorillas'; 'Jackson: Baby stunt was "mistake"'; 'Teenage Jehovah's Witness "died after refusing blood"'.

35. Brighouse and Swift, 'Legitimate parental partiality'.
36. Casal and Williams, 'Equality of resources and procreative justice'.
37. Brighouse and Swift, 'Parents' rights and the value of the family'.
38. Department of Health, *Working Together to Safeguard Children*, 36.
39. Ibid., 37.

6 Sufficiency and Global Justice

Historically, political philosophers have focussed on justice as it applies to individual states or societies. Indeed, Rawls takes this as his starting point for theorising when he states:

> I shall be satisfied if it is possible to formulate a reasonable conception of justice for the basic structure of society conceived for the time being as a closed system isolated from other societies. The significance of this special case is obvious and needs no explanation. It is natural to conjecture that once we have a sound theory for this case, the remaining problems of justice will prove more tractable in the light of it. With suitable modifications such a theory should provide the key for some of these other questions.[1]

More recently, perhaps prompted by increased globalisation, much more attention has been paid to the question of what a just world would look like and what justice-based obligations individuals from one state have to those in another. No doubt a just world would be very unlike our current world. But how, exactly? Would it involve egalitarian redistribution of resources from one nation to another? Or would it simply involve equality within individual states and cordial international relations between them, perhaps with the international community obliged to offer support to greatly burdened societies or only in cases of emergency or extreme poverty?[2] The various positions in global justice debates provide answers to these questions.

In the most general terms, debates about global justice are concerned with who has what sort of obligations of justice to whom and, in particular, whether those living in one state or region have obligations of distributive justice to those living in another state or region. It is not simply a matter of working out what each individual, wherever they are in the world, is owed as a matter of justice, whether that is equality or sufficiency. It also requires an identification of the group or individual who has the substantive responsibility for fulfilling that claim and, in particular, whether those in different states can have responsibility for fulfilling each other's claims.

The positions in this debate have huge implications for, among other things, justice-based reasons to address global poverty and global inequality. This can be explained as follows. If individuals have the same obligations of distributive justice to non-compatriots as they do to compatriots, then all states or individuals ought to equalise, prioritise or sufficientise life prospects, in some dimension, across the world. Such a view promises to turn our current approach to policy selection on its head. We would have to consider the far-flung effects of our policies on non-compatriots as equally relevant to our decision-making as the effects on our compatriots. Giving equal moral weight to the claims of non-compatriots and compatriots alike may lead to declining quality of life in the richest nations of the world as a result of the resource transfers required by justice to improve quality of life elsewhere.

If we have different justice-based obligations to our compatriots than we do to non-compatriots, then this may require us to address only local, but not global, inequality. This would take a potentially onerous set of duties off our plate and would match more closely our current practices where national governments do prioritise the interests of their own citizens. Although international aid is not the only way in which wealthier countries can help much less wealthy countries, it is striking that in 2013 only three countries gave the equivalent of 1 per cent of gross national income in development assistance.[3] However, it is consistent with having different obligations to compatriots and non-compatriots that we owe non-compatriots a great deal and this duty too may be very onerous. Consider, for example, our duties to eradicate world poverty, which may require those in the richest parts of the world to make serious life-style changes – for example, by giving up 10 per cent of their pre-tax income, as one charity suggests.[4]

For these reasons it is worthwhile considering the different views about global justice and assessing their relative plausibility.

Global justice is a major area for debate in distributive justice and it therefore provides an important test for the prospects for sufficientarianism. I have already vindicated two lines of argument for identifying and justifying sufficientarian principles. I have already defended two sufficientarian principles as being indispensable to a complete and sound account of distributive justice. I have also shown that those principles should have an extensive role in our thought about important practical debates. Already we can say that in light of the shift-based characterisation of sufficientarianism, that view looks to have an indispensable and fairly extensive role in our thought about distributive justice.

In this chapter I shift gear a little and focus instead on supporting the claim that sufficientarianism has better prospects than has been thought in global justice, thanks to the shift-based understanding of that view. If the shift-based understanding of sufficientarianism that I have formulated in the opening chapter highlights as yet overlooked but distinctive and plausible positions in this debate, then we can say that the prospects for sufficientarianism are better than has been thought here as well.

My approach in this chapter is not to defend some specific principles as being correct or indispensable to a complete and sound theory of distributive justice, as I have done for other areas of debate in earlier chapters. Rather, my aim is to defend three types of positions that make use of the shift sufficientarian structure set out earlier. I claim that such positions have distinctive advantages over existing sufficientarian and non-sufficientarian accounts of global justice.

Recall that the shift-based understanding that I am defending gives particular content to the broad definition on sufficientarianism, which states that securing enough of some goods is an especially important moral demand. I have argued that the best way of articulating this special importance of securing enough is by saying that securing that amount brings about a change or shift in our non-instrumental reasons to benefit some people further. Securing enough is especially important, on this view, because it makes a difference to how we should regard possible beneficiaries once some have enough.

It is my aim in this chapter to show that this understanding of sufficientarianism makes available distinctive and more plausible positions than are currently defended in debates about global justice. This will be shown at two levels. At the first level, I will show that the positions made available are more plausible than the dominant sufficientarian approaches to global justice, by showing that they avoid the principal objections to those approaches and do not face any additional objections. At the second level, I will show that the positions made available are more plausible in some respects than dominant non-sufficientarian approaches to global justice, by showing that they avoid the principal objections to those approaches and do not face any additional objections. To this end, I set up what I take to be the problem of global justice, that is, determining whether anything and if so what is owed globally and nationally in terms of justice. I also sketch some dominant statist and cosmopolitan positions, including egalitarian, prioritarian and sufficientarian positions, and go on to develop distinctive shift sufficientarian positions. I then show that these distinctive shift sufficientarian positions have important advantages over both the statist and cosmopolitan sufficientarian positions that have been discussed. I then show that these distinctive shift sufficientarian positions have important advantages over both statist and cosmopolitan non-sufficientarian positions that have been discussed. I also discuss at length the unique advantages and attraction of a more radical shift sufficientarian position, which promises to reconcile two conflicting intuitions concerning national partiality and the arbitrariness of state membership.

Global Justice

Some may take it for granted that something like obligations of egalitarian distributive justice apply domestically so then the following two questions are posed:

1. In virtue of what features do people have obligations of justice to one another?
2. How far (beyond the domestic realm) do these features extend?

These questions are important since, if we know what features make some persons have justice-based obligations to others, then we can simply ask whether these features are confined to the domestic realm or if they are common to all persons and thus extend to everyone in the world. More nuanced positions are possible, and these positions would follow from a more scalar view of the features that ground our obligations of justice to others.[5] For example, one such view could hold that the features that ground our obligations of justice vary by the degree to which those features are manifest in the relation between them. On this view, more demanding obligations follow from closer relations and less demanding obligations following from looser relations. A crude version of this view would hold that physical proximity determines the demandingness of our obligations of justice to others and it would follow from this view that my obligation to a person 100 miles away is twice a demanding as my obligation to a person 200 miles away. We can well imagine a more complicated but similar extrapolation from the putatively obligation-grounding features of cooperation or shared culture or values, which may also vary by degree of cooperation or cultural homogeneity.[6] Of course, we still have to define demandingness to know exactly how that could be understood on a sliding scale, but this example illustrates the view clearly enough for now.

Before we endorse these as the relevant two questions, we should note that very few contributors to the debate believe that we have no justice-based obligations to non-compatriots in current and foreseeable circumstances. This is not only because they believe in basic human rights, which generate stringent duties but may not be duties of justice; it is also because it is plausible to believe that the two main grounds of justice, 'cooperation' and 'shared coercive institutions', already hold to some minimal degree between almost all state institutions. Clearly, international trade, international law and domestic actions coordinate the behaviour of people who live in different countries.[7] The immigration laws of countries affect the prospects of neighbouring countries, especially where there are severe inequalities between them. The actions of the World Trade Organization, the European Union, North Atlantic Treaty Organization, the International Monetary Fund and other international institutions organise and regulate global, regional, national and local economies, which themselves profoundly influence the lives of people from different countries in ways that sometimes violate rights, provide some people with no reasonable alternatives but to act in certain ways, and encourage international cooperation. So, it seems that at the very least there is weak cooperation or weak coercion on a global scale. We cannot deny that some of the grounds of justice are manifest in our global relations these days. However, it is worth mentioning that many contributors to this debate reject cooperation or coercion as a ground of justice and have claimed that our common humanity grounds justice. So, the presence of anything more than weak coercion is unnecessary to ground justice for those theorists as well.[8] For this reason, I accept that everyone can owe something as a matter of global justice. Globalisation and increasing interaction have created a world in which the basis for minimal obligations of justice can exist between people wherever they are in the world. Our obligations may vary in accordance with the strength of that cooperation or coercion.[9] Alternatively, the existence of any weak coercion or cooperation may be sufficient for full global justice obligations.

In light of the existence of at least weak justice relations, the two questions we started with do not quite capture what should be the test of the prospects for the shift understanding of sufficientarianism. Our concern is not whether we owe anything at all to non-compatriots, since most reputable positions accept that we do owe something to them. The interesting question is whether what we owe to compatriots is the same as or different from what we owe to non-compatriots. So, for instance, we may have justice-based obligations to all human beings, but the content of these obligations is different depending on whether we share certain features with them, for example, a set of coercive institutions or national history or culture. One example that fits this general structure is the view that we owe very little to non-compatriots and equality to compatriots, but there are many other possible variations and it matters which of these variations is correct. This is the case for at least two reasons. First, these different views have different implications and are vulnerable to different sorts of objections. Second, which view is correct will determine whether we are doing what we ought to or are falling short in terms of distributive justice. For these reasons the above questions are not the ones we should focus on. Instead, we should focus on the following two questions:

3. Do our justice-based obligations to other human beings differ depending on factors that may map onto domestic and international realms?
4. What is the most plausible account of what we owe, whether different or not?

Question three asks whether there is any difference. Those who believe that we have different obligations that roughly track state boundaries are called 'statists'.[10] Those who believe that there are no differences, and that we owe the same to all people in the world, are called 'cosmopolitans'.[11] There are other more nuanced positions that operate on a sliding scale, and we will see that shift sufficientarianism makes some of them available, but for the most part these distinctions will serve us well enough. The fourth question asks what we owe to each group, whether that is the same or different. Candidate answers are given by equality, priority and sufficientarian principles of distributive justice.

In this chapter I will use the term 'shift sufficientarian' to denote views that fit the shift-based understanding of sufficientarianism, which defines any sufficientarian view and is composed of the positive and shift theses, but nevertheless deny the upper limit and headcount claims that make traditional sufficientarian views vulnerable to the objections considered in Chapter 2. My focus here is on the shift sufficientarian positions and their plausibility relative to traditional sufficientarian and non-sufficientarian positions, whether they are statist or cosmopolitan. I am not directly concerned with the moral features that explain that difference, such as coercion, association, etc. The plausibility of any of the positions in this debate depends partly on the explanation for sameness or difference, but it is not one that sufficientarianism, nor shift sufficientarianism, is especially well or badly placed to address. I am interested in developing the shift sufficientarian positions in global justice and drawing attention to the many different, as yet unrecognised roles that sufficiency can play in helping us distinguish our obligations of global justice and local justice, though I will note in my argument several points where I think these shift sufficientarian approaches to global justice do seem to map onto commonly held intuitions that relate to the explanation for sameness or difference.

Shift Sufficientarianism

There are two features with respect to which there may be a difference in our obligations of justice, though there may be more. Each of these features may be described as affecting the *demandingness* of global justice obligations. Shift sufficientarianism prompts us to consider each of these types of difference or demandingness in different ways. Most importantly, shift sufficientarianism prompts us to consider whether our obligations may become different, either more or less demanding, for the reason that one group has secured enough. I explain each difference in more detail below and the way that shift sufficientarian positions use these differences. Recall, the key contention of the shift sufficientarian position is that once a group has secured *enough*, this makes a difference to our reasons to provide further benefits. I will apply this to the differences in our obligations of global distributive justice.

Content

One way in which an obligation can be demanding is in its content, and obligations to different individuals or groups can vary in demandingness in terms of the content of those obligations.

The content of an obligation refers to the conditions under which the obligation has been successfully discharged. If Adam has a duty to pay Bella $10 and Carol $100, then we can say that Adam has different, and differently demanding, duties to Bella and Carol. For example, Adam's duty to pay Carol $100 is more demanding than his duty to pay Bella $10 because fulfilling the duty to Carol is more costly. In the context of global justice debates, a statist might argue that discharging our national obligations to compatriots is more costly (financially or otherwise) than discharging the global obligations, which is only minimal. So, for instance, it is commonly held that individuals owe non-compatriots only a decent standard of living, but that we owe equality, or as high a standard of living as possible, to the least advantaged compatriots. The reason why this is covered by the language of demandingness is that on this sort of view, our obligations appear less demanding than a cosmopolitan egalitarian view.[12] So, the content of the obligation is one way in which our obligations to non-compatriots vary in their demandingness relative to our obligations to compatriots.

There are three ways that shift sufficientarianism can highlight distinctive sufficientarian positions and therefore make a contribution to this debate by applying to the content of our obligations.

Cosmopolitan content shift sufficientarianism
One is a straightforward view, which holds that once any individual has enough, our reasons to benefit them change. This view holds that the content of our cosmopolitan justice-based obligations is simply shift sufficientarian. For example, such a view could hold that we owe diminishing priority to the worse off until everyone secures enough and then we owe equality to all in the world. I call this *cosmopolitan content shift sufficientarianism,* since it denies asymmetry in the content of our obligations to compatriots and non-compatriots (cosmopolitan) and posits sufficiency as a point where our reasons to provide further benefits change, but need not cease (shift sufficientarian). Later, I will argue that these views enjoy all of the advantages over traditional upper limit sufficientarian views that the shift-based understanding of sufficientarianism enjoys in general, such as avoiding the 'indifference objection'.

Statist content shift sufficientarianism

A different set of distinctive shift sufficientarian views would defend shift sufficientarianism either with respect to compatriots, non-compatriots or both, so long as the type of shift in each case were a distinct type of shift. One example is a view that held that our obligations to compatriots resemble uniformly diminishing prioritarianism, until everyone has enough and then we owe them equality, whereas our obligations to non-compatriots are uniformly diminishing, until they have enough, then they diminish at a different rate. This would be a shift sufficientarian view in terms of national and international justice. So long as what we owed to either compatriots or non-compatriots was a version of shift sufficientarianism, this would be a distinctive position.

There are many combinations that the shift makes possible along these lines. What they have in common is that they hold that the content of the obligation to one or both groups (compatriots and non-compatriots) is a version of shift sufficientarianism. I call these views *statist content shift sufficientarianism* because they accept an asymmetry in the content of our obligations (statist), but both sides of that asymmetry are shift sufficientarian, just different types of shift sufficientarianism. These views would be distinct from other statist views in that they could say that whether one group has enough or not affects our reasons to benefit that group further. So, it also enjoys all the benefits of shift sufficientarianism over ordinary sufficientarian and non-sufficientarian views.

Both cosmopolitan content shift sufficientarian and statist content shift sufficientarian views are distinct from other views, including other sufficientarian views, in a fairly straightforward way. They hold that the content of what we owe to one or both of the groups involved (national and international) is shift sufficientarian, whereby what we owe to members of that group changes relative to their achievement of a sufficiency threshold. This confers on these views all of the advantages over traditional sufficientarian views that were discussed in the early chapters. This will be unpacked in more detail, and with reference to specific sufficientarian and non-sufficientarian views below. However, there is a further interesting and, I will argue, plausible application of the shift to differences in our obligations to compatriots and non-compatriots. To complete the survey, a final, and more radical, type of view is made available by the shift-based understanding of sufficientarianism, and this view promises to reconcile some intuitions that prevailing views cannot.

Radical content shift sufficientarianism

In radical content shift sufficientarianism the shift acts not upon the content itself, but rather on whether there is an asymmetry or symmetry in the content of the obligation itself. In other words, whether a person or group has secured enough is going to alter whether we should be statists or cosmopolitans. So, we could owe prioritarianism domestically and sufficiency globally but once some level of sufficiency is reached for one or both groups, we owe equality to all. Rather than triggering a difference in the content of our obligation to members of one group or both, the shift alters the relationship between the content of our obligations to those groups (either by eradicating the difference altogether, or changing the way in which they are different). Thus, the view becomes cosmopolitan in content once enough is secured, but is statist until that level of sufficiency is reached. This peculiar move opens up a number of interesting and, I will argue, plausible positions. I call these views *radical content shift sufficientarianism*.

The key advantage of versions of radical content shift sufficientarianism relative to the traditional sufficientarian upper limit is that they do not need to permit indifference to the global poor once they have secured enough, though this is, of course, shared by the non-radical shift sufficientarian views. The key advantage that versions of radical content shift sufficientarianism have over both non-sufficientarian and non-radical shift sufficientarian approaches is that they promise to reconcile our convictions about the substantive, and not merely formal, equality of all human beings with limited partiality or preference for co-nationals or others with whom we share thicker cultural and cooperative relationships.

Stringency

Another sense in which our obligations can be different, and more demanding, is in terms of the stringency of such obligations. An obligation is more stringent than another if fulfilling that obligation has a very high priority attached to it. So, for instance, if two obligations clashed, we should fulfil the one with the greater stringency. Imagine, again, the case of Adam who has a duty to pay Bella $10 and Carol $100. These duties differ in content, but they may not differ in stringency. If they are equally stringent, then he has no fundamental reason to pay one prior to the other. Imagine, however, that his duty to pay Bella $10 is more stringent than his duty to pay Carol $100, perhaps because he promised to repay Bella first. If Adam can only afford to discharge one duty, then, given its greater stringency, he should pay Bella $10. It is important to note that an obligation can be more demanding in one way – its content (he owes Carol more than Bella) – but less demanding in another important way – its stringency (his duty to Bella is more stringent). If there was an asymmetry with respect to global and national obligations, assuming strict lexical priority, then we should see that national obligations are discharged when both cannot be discharged.

This is an important feature, since we often have scarce resources such that we may benefit either the foreign poor or the domestic poor, but not both. If our domestic obligations were more stringent, even if they had the same content, then we should give priority to benefitting the domestic poor. This does not imply that we owe nothing to non-compatriots, or indeed that we owe them less. It is conceivable that we owe exactly the same, perhaps a level of minimal decency, and that the principles of justice that operate are the same. What it does imply is that non-compatriots' claims come second.

Finally, there can be no non-radical, shift sufficientarian accounts of stringency that are cosmopolitan or statist. Such views would not be distinct from the shift sufficientarian content view. We cannot say that once a person has enough, our obligations become more or less stringent to that co-national, as statists would. To say that simply is to say that the content of our obligation to one co-national changes relative to the content of the obligation to our other co-national and this is just to say that the shift in stringency described here is actually about the content since it is the content, the sufficiency threshold, which triggers it. For this reason, I do not think shift sufficientarian stringency views are a promising group of views for demonstrating the value of thinking about sufficientarianism as a shift-based view, which I am advocating. However, a radical view is possible and may be promising.

Radical stringency shift sufficientarianism

The shift understanding makes available new positions whereby once enough is secured, either domestically or internationally, the relative stringency of our obligations to either group changes. There are at least two types of variation in the stringency of these obligations. First, we could have a view that once we have done enough domestically, our obligations to non-compatriots have priority but our obligations revert to our compatriots once non-compatriots have reached the same or a different level of sufficiency. Second, we could have a view that once we have done enough internationally, our obligations to co-nationals become the most stringent. A third alternative is that once one group has enough, we have no special stringency to either. In essence, once each group has enough, we should endorse cosmopolitanism.

To illustrate how some of these views will work, imagine three levels of advantage, which need not imply the truth of sufficientarianism: poor, well off and opulence. Imagine that we have obligations to improve the position of both co-citizens and of the international community, but how well off any group is, and not the size of the benefit, will determine which obligation is more stringent. So, if co-citizens are poor and the international community is poor, then our obligation to co-citizens is more stringent. However, once co-citizens are well off, and if the international community remains poor, then our obligation to the international community is more stringent than our obligation to others. We can imagine that once the international community is well off, and our co-citizens are well off, then our obligations to co-citizens are more stringent, but when co-citizens enjoy opulence and the international community is well off, then our obligations to the international community are more stringent.

Many variations of the model are possible, with greater or fewer thresholds, or with different priority orderings. So long as securing enough for one of these groups (co-citizens/international community) changes the stringency of our obligations to them, we can say that securing enough makes a difference. And it is a big difference compared with upper limit sufficientarianism.

Note also that the stringency of an obligation can vary *independently* of the content of the obligation. So, we may owe sufficiency at a minimum level to both compatriots and non-compatriots, but sufficiency to compatriots may be more stringent than sufficiency to non-compatriots for reasons of associational ties, shared coercive institutions or some other putative ground of justice. This would be a view where the content of obligations of justice is the same – it seems cosmopolitan – but the stringency is not the same – it seems statist. As such, stringency and content are independent features of our obligations, and specify dimensions along which obligations to different groups can vary. These dimensions can vary for the reason that one group has enough already. This is the work that shift sufficientarianism can do. I call this *radical stringency shift sufficientarianism.*

Few other views in the literature focus on the asymmetry in the stringency of our obligations. Most statist and cosmopolitan positions concern the content of obligations. However, we should note that radical stringency shift sufficientarianism enables us to accommodate two intuitions that are widely shared. These are:

1. Sometimes our obligations to co-nationals are more stringent than our obligations to non-compatriots.
2. The global rich have more stringent duties to alleviate global poverty or inequality than they do to further promote the welfare of compatriots.

My aim is to show that the views that shift sufficientarianism makes available compare favourably with other sufficientarian and non-sufficientarian views in this debate. In particular, I believe the more radical views have distinct advantages over widely discussed sufficientarian and non-sufficientarian positions in the global justice debate. They paint a more complicated picture than we have so far but I think it a more plausible picture of how our justice obligations work in the international context.

Sufficientarian Global Justice

Now that I have developed several distinctive shift sufficientarian positions in the debate about global justice, I must assess whether they are more or less plausible than rival sufficientarian and non-sufficientarian positions in that debate. The first step is to describe the traditional sufficientarian approaches and the main objections to them. I will then show how the new positions can help avoid those objections. Finally, I will respond to some objections that we might have to the shift sufficientarian positions that we would not also have to the traditional sufficientarian positions.[13]

Statism

A widely discussed version of sufficientarianism global justice is offered by David Miller.[14] It holds that the content of obligations of global justice differ depending on whether we share a national history and culture with others. According to this view, if Jon and June share a nationality, they owe each other equality; and if Jon and Diego do not share a nationality, they do not owe each other equality but rather owe each other some kind of minimum threshold of well-being.

What is putatively troubling about this kind of view is first, where you happen to be born seems morally arbitrary in a way that seems to many incapable of justifying enormous disparities in life prospects, even if the worse-off group meets some basic minimum. Second, it seems false to say that we cannot owe anything further to non-compatriots once they have enough, especially if co-nationals can improve the position of non-compatriots without making themselves worse off, for example, by donating unused infrastructure and technology to other countries that could uniquely benefit residents of those other countries because of their climate or current demography. As such, the view suffers from similar problems to upper limit sufficientarianism, which it applies to non-compatriots. These problems can be easily addressed by versions of the non-radical shift sufficientarian views.

Statist content shift sufficientarianism holds that once compatriots have enough, we can still have obligations to non-compatriots but that the content of what we owe is different. This is consistent with attaching some weight to benefitting compatriots and non-compatriots, but with more sharply diminishing weight as they become better off. Such obligations would be a version of uniformly diminishing prioritarianism in content. Consider the following case where this will make a difference:

> Pollution: All countries are minimally well off. Country A is the most well-off country. Due to changes in weather patterns certain types of ultimately degradable waste are created in the river that flows to country B and for which country A is not responsible. As a result the lands of country B are less fertile and there are fewer fish that can be caught in the waters belonging to country B. No one becomes badly off, or poverty stricken, in country B as a result, but they are much worse off than they would have been.

In this case, we can ask, should the residents of country A weigh the costs to country B at all in their decisions about preventing this sort of effect of weather patterns? Would the residents of country B have a valid complaint? I think that the size of the benefits lost by country B matters. Small costs are less important to weigh in our deliberations about what is just. But the fact that this action affects country B is relevant to the decisions country A makes and, with a certain balance of reasons, country A may have an obligation to country B. To deny that such events can trigger obligations of global justice would commit oneself to the view that even enormous, life-changing benefits to the residents of country B would give country A no reason to redesign its foreign aid policy even if doing so made no difference whatsoever to country A's residents, at least where country B is not below some minimal sufficiency threshold.

Sharing a culture, a set of values or forms of coercive institution may be morally relevant and not merely because we tend to be closer to and better able to help those with whom we share values and institutions. But it seems implausible to think that this difference means that those who, by no choice or fault of their own, find themselves in a country that is vulnerable in this way to the actions of others, even above some minimal threshold, can have no complaint when they refuse to confer benefits or alleviate burdens. In this way, the statist shift sufficientarian position avoids an important objection to the statist sufficientarian position. However, we should consider whether this new position is vulnerable to other objections that, all things considered, render the view less plausible.

Let us begin with the attraction of the statist position. If it can be shown that the shift position still has many of the attractions of statism in giving partiality to co-nationals but has one less unattractive feature, we can say that it is more attractive overall. The shift-based understanding does not deprive us of some of the attractions of the statist position. It does not mean that we have to treat non-compatriots on a par with compatriots. Nor does it mean that we must accept huge costs to compatriots in order to provide supra-threshold benefits to non-compatriots. After all, such obligations can be much less stringent. So, I think it captures the main motivation for the statist position and, in addition, avoids a compelling objection to other forms of statism in the form of the indifference objection.

Due to its particular structure, we might think that the shift, rather than the upper limit is unmotivated. The reasons one might give to explain why there is an upper limit would be that we only owe what we owe to non-compatriots on humanitarian grounds.[15] This gives us a satiable reason to benefit them to a point, but no further. The shift sufficientarian view has to maintain that there is some kind of additional, possibly fairly weak, reason that continues to confer weight on benefitting non-compatriots. To respond to this, we could add a concern with global beneficence to our justice-based obligations. We could instead be more politically motivated and concerned with the quality of global or statist democracy rather than well-being. It would make sense of the case above and it would be consonant with the idea of a fairly weak reason operating in the background and one that varies in strength depending on the size of benefit and number of beneficiaries. The motivation for doing so is that we end up with a more plausible account of our obligations of global justice.

I conclude that the shift sufficientarian variant of statism is more plausible than the upper limit sufficientarian variant and so we can say that the prospects for sufficientarianism are better than has been thought. However, it remains to be shown that the shift sufficientarian views are better than other influential views in the literature, including sufficientarian versions of cosmopolitanism. It is to those views that I now turn.

Cosmopolitanism

A cosmopolitan upper limit sufficientarian view would hold that all that global justice demands is that people secure enough and that we owe this equally to compatriots and to non-compatriots. Something like it has been advocated, though not defended, for the purposes of just war theory in Cécile Fabre's *Cosmopolitan War*. The sufficientarian cosmopolitan position is assumed throughout mainly because it is thought that such a view is easier to justify than versions of egalitarianism and so the view is assumed for argument's sake, but one could hold such a view and it would be a sufficientarian view that rivals the shift understanding so it is worthwhile considering its relative merits.

The first thing to note is that this view is vulnerable to the same objections as upper limit sufficientarianism but globally. Sufficientarian cosmopolitanism holds that we do not even have to promote the welfare of our own people once they have enough. This intuition is much less widely shared, as upper limit sufficientarianism is not a widely held position in domestic justice, and Chapter 2 explains why. To illustrate the problematic implications of this view, consider the following example:

Technology: Everyone across the globe has achieved at least a minimal level of welfare and that fact is not going to change. However, significant inequality persists with some individuals just meeting the threshold while others surpass it by some distance. Now, humanity stands on the brink of technological discoveries that are expected to improve everyone's welfare levels and to improve global equality.

The cosmopolitan sufficientarian is genuinely indifferent about whether we ought to make those discoveries or do nothing instead, even when making those discoveries would come at little or no cost. Perhaps we have to simply keep a super-computer running for three more hours to complete some difficult mathematics that will help improve our use of energy and the production of food. The cosmopolitan sufficientarian would be genuinely indifferent, from the point of view of justice, about whether to pull the plug on the super-computer or not. This is simply a version of the indifference objection that makes upper limit sufficientarianism implausible.

Cosmopolitan content shift sufficientarianism can avoid this objection. This is because it can hold that once everyone has secured enough, we should distribute benefits equally or that we should prefer efficiency or benefitting the least advantaged. This view can explain the conviction that we ought to keep the computer plugged in, but non-shift-based views cannot.

So the shift sufficientarian views are more plausible than upper limit sufficientarian views in both the cosmopolitan and statist forms. This demonstrates that the shift makes an important contribution to debates about global justice by making available new positions that are more plausible than the old ones. Shift sufficientarianism therefore makes sufficientarianism a more plausible position than it has been understood to be. However, it remains to be shown whether shift sufficientarianism is a contender in the global justice debate since being a contender in that debate depends not only on its merits relative to other sufficientarian views but also on its merits relative to other influential non-sufficientarian views.

Non-Sufficientarian Global Justice

In this section I want to show that new sufficientarian positions have key advantages relative to dominant non-sufficientarian positions in the debate about global justice. The first step is to describe the dominant non-sufficientarian views of global justice and describe the objections to them. The second step is to describe the shift sufficientarian views and show that they avoid these objections.

I begin by setting out two rival cosmopolitan views:

The Egalitarian Cosmopolitanism View: On this view, all individuals owe all other individuals some form of equality in terms of distributive justice. This is often some version of equality of opportunity, including luck egalitarianism. These views hold that whatever else may be morally relevant, where you are born does not matter and so national boundaries are morally arbitrary and should not influence your life prospects or your access to justice-salient goods.[16]

The Prioritarian Cosmopolitanism View: We ought to prioritise the prospects of the least advantaged in the world, wherever they are, and this priority diminishes as they get better off and only as they get better off – for example, not because they are not co-nationals.[17] The priority either diminishes uniformly or lexical priority is given to the least advantaged group.

Why would anyone have reason to hold a shift sufficientarian cosmopolitan view rather than either of these two views? The answer to this was first given in the earlier chapters that focus on the idea of there being a shift at all. This idea of the shift is motivated by there being at least one satiable reason of justice. The list of autonomy, needs, avoiding deprivation, etc. could support shift sufficientarian cosmopolitanism. So, if you think it is plausible to hold that we have such reasons and if you are already disposed to cosmopolitanism, as proponents of these views are, then these are advantages of shift sufficientarian cosmopolitanism over non-sufficientarian cosmopolitanism.

Moreover, shift sufficientarian cosmopolitanism avoids some further objections that apply to the prioritarian and egalitarian variants. Some object to equality in that it is blind to efficiency gains and could be vulnerable to levelling down. Some object to priority because it is blind to considerations of relative advantage. Versions of shift sufficientarianism can avoid both of these objections, at least in their strongest form. A shift sufficientarian view that was a version of non-uniform prioritarianism would be better able to account for the efficiency gains than an egalitarian cosmopolitan view, though a prioritarian view would also be able to account for these. So, how can we accommodate equality? We can accommodate equality by saying that once everyone has enough, we care about distributing benefits and burdens equally. This helps us resist the levelling down objection in its strongest form, which points out that egalitarians prefer a distribution where everyone is equally badly off to a distribution where everyone is unequally well off. But prioritarianism fares far better with respect to levelling down and to efficiency gains even if it fails in terms of equality. A version of shift sufficientarianism that supports prioritarianism below the threshold and equality above it can accommodate our intuitions about equality, and a shift sufficientarian version of non-uniform prioritarianism can explain our intuition that inequality is less problematic the higher the level of the least advantaged. This demonstrates that shift sufficientarian cosmopolitanism has some advantages in intuitive appeal over some existing cosmopolitan views, but that is not all that shift sufficientarianism has to offer. Radical shift sufficientarian views make available other positions that promise to appeal to those who are pulled in both directions, to some extent. I think these views soften the divide in the debate on global justice and have some distinct advantages.

Radical Views

Recall that on the more radical views one or both group's securing enough has the consequence of changing whether there is a difference in the content or stringency of our obligations to compatriots as opposed to non-compatriots. By contrast, the most straightforward views claim that whether some group has enough or not changes the content or stringency of the obligations.

The radical content shift sufficientarian view holds that whether one group has enough or not can lead to a change in the sameness or difference in the content of the obligations the group has. Possible examples include a view whereby we owe sufficiency to non-compatriots and equality to compatriots but once non-compatriots have enough, we owe equality to all. Thus, the view moves from being a minimalist upper limit sufficientarian statist view to a cosmopolitan egalitarian or prioritarian view once everyone has secured enough. Straightforward views recommend no such change once enough is secured.

The radical stringency shift sufficientarian view holds that whether our obligations to compatriots are equally stringent or differently stringent from our obligations to non-compatriots depends on whether one group has enough. Possible examples include a view whereby our obligations to promote the well-being of co-nationals have priority over our obligations to promote the well-being of non-compatriots, but once co-nationals have enough, the obligations become equally stringent and compatriots have no particular priority. As such, the view becomes cosmopolitan in terms of stringency of obligations once compatriots have enough, but prior to that it is distinctly statist.

The distinct advantage of radical content shift sufficientarianism over other versions of sufficientarianism is that we can have serious ongoing obligations to others throughout the world and that there is still some important difference in what we owe or in the priority of that obligation for co-nationals. So, it does not deny the importance of national citizenship, culture or reciprocity. It merely restricts those reasons' scope to alter rather than completely change our obligations. Moreover, the level of well-being of certain members does seem to track our intuitions about the injustice of global inequality and not simply global poverty.

The distinct advantage of radical content shift sufficientarianism over cosmopolitan views is that they are more statist and the advantage over statist views is that they are more cosmopolitan. They allow some scope for national partiality, but without the upper limit sufficientarian implication of indifference to the relative position of non-compatriots.

Many theorists are drawn to the view that there is some kind of priority that should be given to compatriots. The idea is that shared national culture, living under the same coercive institutions or simply interacting much more often with certain people can justify some preference for the promotion of their interests. Call this 'Compatriot Partiality'.[18] This conviction gains some support from plausible claims of partiality in other areas of morality too, such as in the morality of the family.[19] The relevance of partiality may be particularly strong when those we might benefit instead of those we are partial to are already sufficiently well off. Partiality appears to be particularly weak justification when members we could benefit are themselves well off but non-members who may benefit are very badly off.

Many people are also drawn to the view that sometimes we ought to minimise global inequality or improve the position of the global poor, at the cost of improving the lives of compatri-ots. They are doubtful that the reasons that ground compatriot partiality are strong enough to justify neglect for the global poor, even if they are above some minimal threshold.[20] Cosmopolitans often argue that compatriot partiality cannot be justified because individuals are not responsible and have no control over where they are born and the strength of that country's economy relative to others. Thomas Pogge states the intuition in a compelling way: 'Nationality is just one further deep contingency (like genetic endowment, race, gender, and social class), one more potential basis of institutional inequalities that are inescapable and present from birth.'[21] As such, nationality, citizenship, etc. are just as arbitrary as the contingencies whose effects many liberal theories of justice seek to eliminate. As such, these features cannot justify individuals being worse off than others as a result. Call this 'State is Arbitrary'.[22]

On the face of it, these intuitions seem to be in tension. It goes some way to explaining the polarisation of the debate that individuals have gone one way or the other. Statists hold that Compatriot Partiality is the more strongly held conviction. Cosmopolitans hold that State is Arbitrary is the more strongly held conviction. Of course, the debate between the positions is not simply determined by the stronger intuition. The rationales for each position are sought and they themselves have an intuitive pull, one way or another. But the motivation for the need to rigor-ously test the rationales of each position comes from accepting the seeming incompatibility of the two intuitions. If the two intuitions are not incompatible, this opens up different positions that also ought to be tested. Shift sufficientarianism opens them up along sufficientarian lines whereby the two intuitions can be reconciled, in a limited way, by appeal to a sufficiency threshold.

If taken in their extreme form, the intuitions are incompatible. If Compatriot Partiality is the view that claims of compatriots always trump any claims that non-compatriots have beyond some basic needs, and if State is Arbitrary is the view that it is never reasonable to give extra weight to or to treat differently others because of factors that they cannot control, such as nationality or the degree of interaction they have with others, then the two are flatly incompatible. This is because Compatriot Partiality is premised on there being some feature of compatriots, necessarily beyond control, that is not arbitrary but means we should treat compatriots differently from others. State is Arbitrary is premised on the thought that there are no grounds for partiality with respect to compatriots. However, I do not think we have most reason to think that our intuitions are best captured by these general claims. Rather, I think they are best captured by slightly weaker claims, and these weaker claims are compatible with each other and shift sufficientarianism offers a plausible reconciliation of them.

Consider now 'Weak Compatriot Partiality': sometimes we have at least some reason to prioritise the interests of compatriots, or at least to think that we sometimes owe them something quite different from what is owed to others. Consider also 'Weak State is Arbitrary': sometimes we have at least some reason to not prioritise the interests of compatriots, or at least to think that we sometimes owe them the same as what we owe to everyone else.

These views are compatible because we can sometimes give partiality to compatriots and sometimes treat them exactly the same. The tricky part is identifying a non-arbitrary pivot. A sufficiency threshold can play this role and the nature of the reasons that apply can help us to explain. The nature of these reasons can be in terms of the stringency, or content or both. As such, a shift sufficientarian approach can be more plausible with respect to both intuitions and this is what recommends it as an approach to global justice. It can favour Weak Compatriot Partiality by insisting that until sufficiency is achieved, compatriots have priority; and it can endorse a weak version of State is Arbitrary by insisting that we do still have important obligations to non-compatriots, which can themselves trump our domestic obligations once we have secured enough for compatriots.

Conclusion

In this chapter I have argued that shift sufficientarianism renders the prospects for sufficientarianism as an approach to debates on global justice seriously improved. I started arguing that there are straightforward shift sufficientarian positions that are more plausible than traditional sufficientarian positions in global justice. I did so by showing that the shift sufficientarian positions could avoid objections to which the traditional views were vulnerable and that the shift sufficientarian positions faced no additional objections. I then went on to show that the straightforward shift sufficientarian positions had key advantages over non-sufficientarian positions in global justice. I did so by showing that the shift sufficientarian positions could avoid objections to which these non-sufficientarian views were vulnerable and that the shift sufficientarian positions faced no additional objections. Finally, I considered a number of radical shift sufficientarian positions that are rather promising because they help to capture two commonly held intuitions. First, they need not insist that what we owe to non-compatriots is only minimal and can be sated. Second, they can accommodate the intuition that there is some kind of asymmetry and so we need not be cosmopolitans in stringency, content or either. In other words, these positions help to reconcile the statist and cosmopolitan intuitions. This chapter completes my defence of the prospects for sufficientarianism in light of the shift-based characterisation of sufficientarianism.

Notes

1. Rawls, *A Theory of Justice*, 7.
2. The notion of burdened societies and the view described in this question is similar to one espoused in Rawls, *The Law of People*.
3. See figures from OECD, 'Aid to developing countries'.
4. See Giving What We Can, <https://www.givingwhatwecan.org/about-us/history> (last accessed 17 March 2016).
5. This is suggested in Julius, 'Nagel's atlas'.
6. These features are widely thought to count singly or collectively as grounds of justice. See, for example, Rawls, *The Law of Peoples*; Miller, *Globalizing Justice*; Blake, 'Distributive justice, state coercion, and autonomy'; Nagel, 'The problem of global justice'; Cohen and Sabel, 'Extra rempublicam nulla justitia?'; Beitz, 'Justice and international relations'; Pogge, 'Rawls and global justice'; Miller, *On Nationality*; Sangiovanni, 'Global justice, reciprocity, and the state'.
7. Some have doubted that international trade alone can ground obligations of justice between trading communities. See Barry, 'Humanity and justice in global perspective'.
8. Caney, *Justice Beyond Borders*; Tan, *Justice Without Borders*; Gilabert, *From Global Poverty to Global Equality*; Nussbaum, *Frontiers of Justice*; Sen, *Development as Freedom*; Singer, 'Famine, affluence, and morality'.
9. As argued for in Cohen and Sabel, 'Extra rempublicam nulla justitia?' and Julius, 'Nagel's atlas'.
10. Blake, 'Distributive justice, state coercion, and autonomy'; Goodin, 'What is so special about our fellow countrymen?'; Miller, *On Nationality*; Miller, *Global Justice and National Responsibility*; Nagel, 'The problem of global justice'; Rawls, *The Law of Peoples*.
11. Abizadeh, *Citizenship, Immigration and Boundaries*; Arneson, 'Do patriotic ties limit global justice duties?'; Brock, *Global Justice*; Caney, *Justice Beyond Borders*; Cohen and Sabel, 'Extra rempublicam nulla justitia?; Gilabert, *From Global Poverty to Global Equality*; Nussbaum, *Frontiers of Justice*; Tan, *Justice Without Borders*; Unger, *Living High and Letting Die*.
12. However, it is possible for obligations of equality to be met much more easily than obligations of sufficiency. This is particularly so if levelling down is available and if the sufficiency level is quite high.
13. For discussion of the usefulness of sufficiency thresholds in debates

about global justice, see Casal, 'Global taxes on natural resources'; Pogge, 'Allowing the poor to share the earth'.

14. Blake, 'Distributive justice, state coercion, and autonomy'; Miller, *On Nationality*; Miller, *Global Justice and National Responsibility*; Nagel, 'The problem of global justice'; Rawls, *The Law of Peoples*; Goodin, 'What is so special about our fellow countrymen?'

15. Nagel, 'The problem of global justice'.

16. See Altman and Wellman, *A Liberal Theory of International Justice*; Brock, *Global Justice*; Steiner, 'Territorial justice and global redistribution'; Tan, 'Luck, institutions, and global distributive justice'.

17. See Holtug, 'The cosmopolitan strikes back'; Moellendorf, 'The World Trade Organization and egalitarian justice'; Pogge, *Realizing Rawls*.

18. Goodin, 'What is so special about our fellow countrymen?'; Miller, 'Reasonable partiality towards compatriots'; Miller, *Globalizing Justice*.

19. Brighouse and Swift, 'Legitimate parental partiality'; Schoeman, 'Rights of children, rights of parents, and the moral basis of the family'.

20. For a recent discussion of this view, which the author calls 'The concerned rich person's view', see Child, 'The global justice gap'.

21. Pogge, *Realizing Rawls*, 247.

22. Caney, *Justice Beyond Borders*; Carens, 'Refugees and the limits of obligation'; Pogge, *Realizing Rawls*; Tan, *Justice Without Borders*.

7 Conclusion

In this book I have argued that we should be optimistic about the prospects for sufficientarianism and the role that sufficientarianism has in a complete and sound account of justice. I have explained that even though two powerful objections can be made to the two most prominent versions of sufficientarianism, these versions of sufficientarianism relied upon extreme claims that sufficientarians need not make. I set out a characterisation of the minimum claims that one would have to make in order to hold a distinctive sufficientarian view. I have referred to this as a shift-based understanding of sufficientarianism, and the chapters of this book have defended the principles made available by this understanding as being more plausible than rival principles in a variety of areas. More specifically, I have argued that two sufficientarian principles, the principle of sufficient autonomy and the principle of a good enough upbringing, are indispensable to a complete and sound theory of distributive justice and should have an extensive role in our thought about practical debates about educational fairness and child custody, respectively. In addition, I have argued that the shift sufficientarian approach makes available positions in the global distributive justice debate that are more promising than traditional sufficientarian approaches and non-sufficientarian approaches. In this Conclusion I will briefly restate my main claims before considering what the future holds for sufficientarianism.

Main Claims

The main argument of the book began in Chapter 2 by considering what the prospects for sufficientarianism consist in. I have claimed that the prospects for sufficientarianism are a function of, roughly, three factors. These are:

1. the degree to which sufficientarian principles are indispensable;
2. the extent of the role these principles play in our thought about practical debates;
3. the number of these principles.

With this in mind, I claimed that the first task in examining the prospects for sufficientarianism was to see if there were any indispensable principles of sufficiency since, if we could do without them and get the most plausible guidance, then there would be no reason to be optimistic about principles of sufficiency having a role in a sound and complete account of distributive justice. Having done so, I claimed that indispensable principles of distributive justice are those that are distinctive and more plausible than their rivals.

I then sought to examine the prospects for sufficientarianism by appealing to these factors based on a review of the main literature on the topic. I made a series of claims about how we can divide up this literature in general terms. I claimed that the versions of sufficientarianism that can be found in the literature can be divided into two camps. There are versions of what I call 'headcount sufficientarianism' and there are versions of what I call 'upper limit sufficientarianism'. Headcount sufficientarians make the headcount claim, which states that 'we should maximise the number of people who have secured *enough*'. Upper limit sufficientarians make the upper limit claim, which states that 'once people have secured *enough*, no distributive criteria apply to benefitting them'. I then claimed, in agreement with much of the critical literature, that both of these versions of sufficientarianism are vulnerable to powerful objections in virtue of their central claims. Versions of headcount sufficientarianism are vulnerable to the upwards transfers objection, which states that it is implausible to permit benefitting the better off by tiny amounts instead of benefitting the worse off by very large but insufficient amounts. Versions of upper limit sufficientarianism are vulnerable to what I call the 'objectionable indifference objection', which states that it is implausible to be indifferent about the way benefits and burdens are shared once individuals have secured enough. Versions of upper limit sufficientarianism, I claimed, could avoid this objection only by raising the threshold so high that they would also be sacrificing what makes them distinctive. I concluded that since almost all sufficientarian principles hitherto advocated have been one of these two versions of sufficientarianism, and since both versions are either less plausible than their rivals or fail to be distinctive, the prospects for sufficientarianism seem bleak.

I then raised the question of whether the objections that had been made of sufficientarian principles must apply to all distinctive sufficientarian principles. I began to consider what a distinctive sufficientarian principle must claim. I argued that a distinctive sufficientarian principle must make the following claims:

The Positive Thesis: We have weighty non-instrumental reasons to secure at least enough of some good(s).

The Shift Thesis: Once people have secured enough, there is a discontinuity in the rate of change of the marginal weight of our reasons to benefit them further.

Putting these together, I claimed that we can say that the distinctive sufficientarian position is defined by the claim that providing people with enough is important and that once people have secured enough, our reasons for benefitting them further change. Since the positive and shift theses are definitive of distinctive sufficientarian principles, and since the prospects for sufficientarianism depend upon the relative plausibility of distinctive sufficientarian principles, I claimed that the prospects for sufficientarianism depend upon the plausibility of the positive and shift theses together. Moreover, I claimed that, so characterised, versions of sufficientarianism could avoid the objections that had been made of them and so we should re-examine the prospects for sufficientarianism.

I then claimed that there were at least two ways that we might argue for sufficientarian principles and identify debates in which sufficientarian principles are going to be plausible. The first way of arguing for sufficientarian principles I described as identifying sufficientarian reasons. I claimed that sufficientarian reasons could support the idea that a shift takes place in our reasons to benefit people once they have secured enough. Since the shift is a distinctive claim of sufficientarian principles, wherever we have shifts we require sufficientarian principles. Sufficientarian reasons, I claimed, are weighty, non-instrumental, non-egalitarian and satiable. The second way that we can argue for sufficientarian principles, and identify debates in which sufficientarian principles are going to be plausible, I described as the value clash argument. The idea behind this line of argument is that wherever there are two values, interests or claims that clash, and that seem unavoidable, one plausible resolution will be to state that once one value, interest or claim is satisfied to sufficient extent, the other value, interest or claim becomes relatively more important. This solution can be contrasted with either rejecting the value conflict or else giving lexical priority to one value.

In Chapter 3, I claimed that the principle of sufficient autonomy, which states that we have weighty, non-instrumental, non-egalitarian and satiable reasons to secure sufficient autonomy for the conditions of freedom, is indispensable to a complete and sound theory of distributive justice. I used sufficientarian reasons to argue for this principle and in doing so vindicated this line of argument as one capable of identifying and supporting sufficientarian principles.

In Chapter 4, I claimed that the principle of sufficient autonomy should have an extensive role in our thought about debates about justice and educational provision. I did so by claiming that the principle can help us in debates about opting out of state education and helped to correct a defect with John Rawls's principle of fair equality of opportunity. This supported the overall conclusion that the prospects for sufficientarianism are good. I also showed that the principle of sufficient autonomy has more plausible implications than two prominent sufficientarian approaches to justice in education.

In Chapter 5, I claimed that the principle of a good enough upbringing was indispensable to a complete and sound theory of distributive justice and that if a parent was providing a child with a good enough upbringing, he or she could not usually be denied custody of that child. I also went on to show that this principle should have an extensive role in our thought as it has important implications for debates about justice and policy.

In Chapter 6, I devised a number of shift sufficientarian approaches to our different obligations of global justice to compatriots and non-compatriots, and I argued that these approaches had advantages over traditional sufficientarian and non-sufficientarian approaches.

The Future for Sufficientarianism

In this final section I will discuss briefly what difference my main claims have made to the debate about the role of considerations of sufficiency in debates about justice and then I will offer some thoughts about future research in this area.

My aim in this book was to show that in distributive justice considerations of sufficiency are much more useful than had been shown and are in fact indispensable if we are to have sound guidance. When I began this research, I believed that sufficientarianism was widely regarded as a highly problematic way of thinking about distributive justice. The existence of several compelling objections, repeated by many excellent philosophers, to the two main versions of sufficientarianism vindicates that thought. I believe that I have in some ways given sufficientarianism its due, that is to say, I believe that I have presented the most charitable and philosophically rigorous general account of sufficientarianism, an account that relies on a shift in our reasons once enough is secured. I have used this characterisation to highlight that we need to use considerations of sufficiency in thinking about justice. In articulating the shift thesis and the positive thesis together I believe that I have made it easier to answer the question 'What, if any, role can considerations of sufficiency play in distributive justice?' I have elaborated an account of sufficientarianism that explains exactly what is at stake in debates between sufficientarians and their critics. My hope is that political philosophers will look at debates in distributive justice and will see sufficiency as a putative answer worthy of consideration, rather than as an answer that invites several powerful and long-standing objections. The main claims I have made about the characterisation of sufficientarianism and the lines of argument that we can use to identify where, if anywhere, sufficientarianism might be a plausible approach to questions of distributive justice should be helpful to others. These claims are non-partisan. You do not need to be a sufficientarian to appreciate a clearer characterisation of that view. Any conscientious philosopher working in distributive justice will appreciate a clearer target. It is for these reasons that I believe that these claims will be the main contribution of this book.

The claims that I make in Chapters 2–5 are crucial to rescuing sufficientarianism from disrepute. I hope they also make important contributions to various debates independently of their attachments to that task. The conditions of belief formation pose a significant problem for those views that do not accept the principle of sufficient autonomy. The principle also has important implications for practice as well as theory, as Chapter 3 shows. The account of the good enough upbringing I defend in Chapter 4 is highly significant to a number of important issues and is not restricted in its importance only to debates about removing children from the custody of their parents. It sets a real goal for policy that affects children. Furthermore, the principle of a good enough upbringing suggests a point beyond which it may be unreasonable to require non-parents to share in the burdens of child-rearing. Another suggestion, which was not addressed in this book, is that this standard of a good enough upbringing could apply globally and thus could help to guide and assess international adoption, most notably practised by various celebrities. But that principle has wider significance than in helping us to make sound judgements about celebrities. In a world where one's country of birth has such a radical influence on one's life chances, international adoption, from a poor to a rich country, may be obligatory, let alone permissible. I do not claim that the account of the good enough upbringing can do all of this work, and I do not need to in order to establish my conclusion, but I hope to have something to say about this in the future. In any case, whatever the correct standard in those important areas, the work in Chapter 5 should prove instructive as it seems likely the criteria I develop in that chapter will apply to those same decisions since there is a clash of the child's and parent's interests.

I now wish to say something about the future for sufficientarianism itself. It is perhaps too much to hope that political philosophers will accept that our reasons of justice are often non-instrumental and satiable in terms of the weight they confer on claims for additional resources. Having said that, it is clear, to me at least, that political philosophers interested in distributive justice must consider sufficiency more seriously and I hope that it will be taken up in several debates, if not as the solution to a problem, then at least as one contender that must be engaged with. More specifically, I believe that sufficientarianism will have a prominent role in debates about non-ideal theory and about consensus. It seems that in non-ideal theory we are interested in setting interim goals that can be achieved. Though I cannot provide a defence of this claim here, I believe that satiable, non-instrumental, non-egalitarian goals will be more plausible than others. Moreover, it seems that sufficientarian principles may be able to garner a greater degree of consensus and therefore have a claim to greater legitimacy than rival principles. I briefly discussed one possible application of this reasoning in Chapter 4. In this book I have argued mainly that sufficientarian principles have an indispensable role in debates about children and education, but I believe we can fruitfully look at debates in health and in taxation more closely too. I consider this to be the subject of future research.

Finally, I hope that in the future sufficientarianism and egalitarianism will have a more convivial relationship. I have accepted that equality and sufficiency need not be mutually exclusive positions, indeed I have argued that sufficientarianism is best understood as a complementary demand of justice, and that a commitment to social egalitarianism, understood as the claim that individuals should have equal standing in society, may plausibly require attaching special importance to securing enough. There is more to be said about this relationship, and it should be easier to say now that we have a clear account of what sufficientarianism is. I hope that in the future this relationship can be elucidated as I believe it is of considerable importance.[1]

Note

1. Some have already explored some possibilities such as Casal, 'Why sufficiency is not enough'; Axelsen and Nielsen, 'Sufficiency as freedom from duress'.

Bibliography

Abizadeh, A., *Citizenship, Immigration and Boundaries* (Oxford: Oxford University Press, 2010).

Altman, A. and C. H. Wellman, *A Liberal Theory of International Justice* (Oxford: Oxford University Press, 2009).

Anderson, E., 'What is the point of equality?', *Ethics*, 109 (2) 1999, pp. 287–337.

Anderson, E., 'Rethinking equality of opportunity: comment on Adam Swift's "How not to be a hypocrite"', *Theory and Research in Education*, 2 (2) 2004, pp. 323–42.

Anderson, E., 'Fair opportunity in education: a democratic equality perspective', *Ethics*, 117 (4) 2007, pp. 595–622.

Archard, D., 'Children, multiculturalism, and education', in D. Archard and C. M. Macleod (eds), *The Moral and Political Status of Children* (Oxford: Oxford University Press, 2002), pp. 142–59.

Archard, D. and C. M. Macleod (eds), *The Moral and Political Status of Children* (Oxford: Oxford University Press, 2002).

Arneson, R., 'Against Rawlsian equality of opportunity', *Philosophical Studies*, 93 (1) 1999, pp. 77–112.

Arneson, R., 'Perfectionism and politics', *Ethics*, 111 (1) 2000, pp. 37–63.

Arneson, R., 'Welfare should be the currency of justice', *Canadian Journal of Philosophy*, 30 (4) 2000, pp. 497–524.

Arneson, R., 'Distributive justice and basic capability equality: "good enough" is not good enough', in A. Kaufman (ed.), *Capabilities Equality: Basic Issues and Problems* (Oxford: Routledge, 2005), pp. 17–43.

Arneson, R., 'Do patriotic ties limit global justice duties?, *The Journal of Ethics*, 9 (1–2) 2005, pp. 127–50.

Arneson, R. and I. Shapiro, 'Democratic autonomy and religious liberty: a critique of Wisconsin v. Yoder', in R. Hardin and I. Shapiro (eds),

NOMOS XXXVIII: Political Order (New York: New York University Press, 1996), pp. 365–411.

Axelsen, D. and L. Nielsen, 'Sufficiency as freedom from duress', *Journal of Political Philosophy*, 23 (4) 2015, pp. 406–26.

Barry, B., 'Humanity and justice in global perspective', in J. Pennock and J. Chapman (eds), *NOMOS XXIV: Ethics, Economics and the Law* (New York: New York University Press, 1982), pp. 219–52.

'BBC Profile: Josef Fritzl', BBC News, <http://news.bbc.co.uk/1/hi/7371959.stm> (last accessed 17 March 2016).

Beitz, C., 'Justice and international relations', *Philosophy and Public Affairs*, 4 (4) 1975, pp. 360–89.

Beitz, C., *Political Theory and International Relations* (Princeton, NJ: Princeton University Press, 1999).

Benbaji, Y., 'The doctrine of sufficiency: a defence', *Utilitas*, 17 (3) 2005, pp. 310–32.

Benbaji, Y., 'Sufficiency or priority?', *European Journal of Philosophy*, 14 (3) 2006, pp. 327–48.

Blake, M., 'Distributive justice, state coercion, and autonomy', *Philosophy and Public Affairs*, 30 (3) 2001, pp. 257–96.

Brennan, S., 'The intrinsic goods of childhood', blog post, 20 April 2007, <http://peasoup.typepad.com/peasoup/2007/04/the_intrinsic_g.html> (last accessed 17 March 2016).

Brighouse, H., *On Education* (Oxford: Routledge, 2006).

Brighouse, H. and A. Swift, 'Equality, priority and positional goods', *Ethics*, 116 (3) 2006, pp. 471–97.

Brighouse, H. and A. Swift, 'Parents' rights and the value of the family', *Ethics*, 117 (1) 2006, pp. 80–108.

Brighouse, H. and A. Swift, 'Educational equality versus educational adequacy: a critique of Anderson and Satz', *Journal of Applied Philosophy*, 26 (2) 2009, pp. 117–28.

Brighouse, H. and A. Swift, 'Legitimate parental partiality', *Philosophy and Public Affairs*, 37 (1) 2009, pp. 43–80.

Brighouse, H. and A. Swift, *Family Values: The Ethics of Parent–Child Relationships* (Princeton: Princeton University Press, 2014).

Brock, G., *Global Justice: A Cosmopolitan Account* (Oxford: Oxford University Press, 2009).

Brown, C., 'Priority or sufficiency . . . or both?', *Economics and Philosophy*, 21 (2) 2005, pp. 199–220.

Callan, E., 'Autonomy, child-rearing, and good lives', in D. Archard and C. M. Macleod (eds), *The Moral and Political Status of Children* (Oxford: Oxford University Press, 2002), pp. 118–41.

Caney, S., *Justice Beyond Borders: A Global Political Theory* (Oxford: Oxford University Press, 2005).

Carens, J., 'Refugees and the limits of obligation', *Public Affairs Quarterly*, 6 (1) 1992, pp. 31–44.

Casal, P., 'Why sufficiency is not enough', *Ethics*, 117 (2) 2007, pp. 296–326.

Casal, P., 'Global taxes on natural resources', *Journal of Moral Philosophy* 8 (3) 2011, pp. 307–27.

Casal, P. and A. Williams, 'Equality of resources and procreative justice', in J. Burley (ed.), *Dworkin and His Critics* (Oxford: Blackwell, 2004), pp. 150–69.

Child, R., 'The global justice gap', *Critical Review of International Social and Political Philosophy* (forthcoming).

Christiano, T., 'A foundation for egalitarianism', in N. Holtug and K. Lippert-Rasmussen (eds), *Egalitarianism: New Essays on the Nature and Value of Equality* (Oxford: Oxford University Press, 2006), pp. 41–82.

Christman, J., 'Constructing the inner citadel: recent work on autonomy', *Ethics*, 99 (1) 1988, pp. 109–24.

Christman, J. and J. Anderson (eds), *Autonomy and the Challenges to Liberalism* (Cambridge: Cambridge University Press, 2005).

Clayton, M., *Justice and Legitimacy in Upbringing* (Oxford: Oxford University Press, 2006).

Cohen, G. A., 'On the currency of egalitarian justice', *Ethics*, 99 (4) 1989, pp. 906–44.

Cohen, G. A., *Rescuing Justice and Equality* (London: Harvard University Press, 2008).

Cohen, J. and C. Sabel, 'Extra rempublicam nulla justitia?', *Philosophy and Public Affairs*, 34 (2) 2006, pp. 147–75.

Crisp, R., 'Equality, priority, and compassion', *Ethics*, 113 (4) 2003, pp. 745–63.

Crisp, R., 'Egalitarianism and compassion', *Ethics*, 114 (1) 2003, pp. 119–26.

Crisp, R., 'Well-being', in E. N. Zalta (ed.), *The Stanford Encyclopedia of Philosophy (Fall 2008 edition)*, <http://plato.stanford.edu/archives/win2008/entries/well-being/> (last accessed 17 March 2016).

Curren, R., 'Justice and the threshold of educational equality', in M. Katz (ed.), *Philosophy of Education*, 50 1995, pp. 239–48.

Department of Health, *Working Together to Safeguard Children: A Guide to Inter-agency Working to Safeguard and Promote the Welfare of Children* (London: The Stationery Office, 2006), <http://

webarchive.nationalarchives.gov.uk/20130401151715/http://www.
education.gov.uk/publications/eOrderingDownload/WT2006%20
Working_together.pdf> (last accessed 25 March 2016).

Dorsey, D., 'Toward a theory of the basic minimum', *Politics, Philosophy & Economics*, 7 (4) 2008, pp. 423–45.

Dworkin, G., *The Theory and Practice of Autonomy* (Cambridge: Cambridge University Press, 1988).

Dworkin, R., *Sovereign Virtue* (London: Harvard University Press, 2001).

Fabre, C., *Cosmopolitan War* (Oxford: Oxford University Press, 2012).

Fleurbaey, M., *Fairness, Responsibility, and Welfare* (Oxford: Oxford University Press, 2008).

Frankfurt, H., 'Equality as a moral ideal', *Ethics*, 98 (1) 1987, pp. 21–43.

Gheaus, A., 'The right to parent one's biological baby', *Journal of Political Philosophy*, 20 (4) 2011, pp. 432–55.

Gilabert, P., *From Global Poverty to Global Equality: A Philosophical Exploration* (Oxford: Oxford University Press, 2012).

Goodin, R., 'What is so special about our fellow countrymen?', *Ethics*, 98 (4) 1988, pp. 663–86.

Gutmann, A., *Democratic Education* (Princeton, NJ: Princeton University Press, 1987).

Hannan, S. and R. Vernon, 'Parental rights: a role-based approach', *Theory and Research in Education*, 6 (2) 2008, pp. 173–89.

Hirose, I., 'Reconsidering the value of equality', *Australasian Journal of Philosophy*, 87 (2) 2009, pp. 301–12.

Holtug, N., 'Prioritarianism', in N. Holtug and K. Lippert-Rasmussen (eds), *Egalitarianism: New Essays on the Nature and Value of Equality* (Oxford: Oxford University Press, 2006), pp. 125–55.

Holtug, N., 'The cosmopolitan strikes back: a critical discussion of Miller on nationality and global equality', *Ethics & Global Politics*, 4 (3) 2011, pp. 147–63.

Hooker, B., 'Fairness, needs and desert', in B. Colburn, C. Grant, A. Hatzistavrou and M. Kramer (eds), *The Legacy of H. L. A. Hart: Legal, Political and Moral Philosophy* (Oxford: Oxford University Press, 2008), pp. 181–99.

Huseby, R., 'Sufficiency: restated and defended', *Journal of Political Philosophy*, 18 (2) 2010, pp. 178–97.

Huxley, A., *Brave New World* (New York: Harper, 1932).

'Jackson: Baby stunt was "mistake"', BBC News, <http://news.bbc.

co.uk/1/hi/entertainment/2494249.stm> (last accessed 17 March 2016).

Julius, A. J., 'Nagel's atlas', *Philosophy and Public Affairs*, 34 (2) 2006, pp. 176–92.

Kanschik, P., 'Why sufficientarianism is not indifferent to taxation', *Kriterion*, 29 (2) 2015, pp. 81–102.

Kekes, J., 'A question for egalitarians', *Ethics*, 107 (4) 1997, pp. 658–69.

Lamont, J. and C. Favor, 'Distributive justice', in E. N. Zalta (ed.), *The Stanford Encyclopedia of Philosophy (Fall 2008 edition)*, <http://plato.stanford.edu/archives/fall2008/entries/justice-distributive> (last accessed 17 March 2016).

Liao, S. M., 'The right of children to be loved', *Journal of Political Philosophy*, 14 (4) 2006, pp. 420–40.

Macleod, C. M., 'Primary goods, capabilities, and children', in H. Brighouse and I. Robeyns (eds), *Measuring Justice* (Cambridge: Cambridge University Press, 2010), pp. 174–92.

Mason, A., 'Equality, personal responsibility and gender socialisation', *Proceedings of the Aristotelian Society*, 100 (1) 2000, pp. 227–46.

Miller, D., *On Nationality* (Oxford: Oxford University Press, 1995).

Miller, D., 'Reasonable partiality towards compatriots', *Ethical Theory and Moral Practice*, 8 (1) 2005, pp. 63–81.

Miller, D., *Global Justice and National Responsibility* (Oxford: Oxford University Press, 2007).

Miller, R., *Globalizing Justice: The Ethics of Poverty and Power* (Oxford: Oxford University Press, 2010).

Moellendorf, D., 'The World Trade Organization and egalitarian justice', *Metaphilosophy*, 36 (1–2) 2005, pp. 145–62.

Nagel, T., 'The problem of global justice', *Philosophy and Public Affairs*, 33 (2) 2005, pp. 113–47.

Nielsen, L., 'Sufficiency grounded as sufficiently free: a reply to Shlomi Segall', *Journal of Applied Philosophy*, online first: DOI: 10.1111/japp.12159.

Noggle, D., 'Special agents: children's autonomy and parental authority', in D. Archard and C. M. Macleod (eds), *The Moral and Political Status of Children* (Oxford: Oxford University Press, 2002), pp. 97–117.

Nozick, R., *Anarchy, State, Utopia* (Oxford: Blackwell, 1974).

Nussbaum, M., *Women and Human Development: The Capabilities Approach* (Cambridge: Cambridge University Press, 2002).

Nussbaum, M., *Frontiers of Justice: Disability, Nationality, Species Membership* (London: Harvard University Press, 2009).

OECD, 'Aid to developing countries rebounds in 2013 to reach an all-time high', <http://www.oecd.org/newsroom/aid-to-developing-coun tries-rebounds-in-2013-to-reach-an-all-time-high.htm> (last accessed 17 March 2016).

O'Neill, M., 'What should egalitarians believe?', *Philosophy and Public Affairs*, 36 (2) 2008, pp. 119–56.

Orr, S. W., 'Sufficiency of resources and political morality', paper presented at the Priority in Practice seminars, 22–3 September 2005, University College London, <http://www.ucl.ac.uk/~ucesswo/ Sufficiency%20of%20Resources%202.doc> (last accessed 25 March 2016).

Page, E., *Climate Change, Justice and Future Generations* (Cheltenham: Edward Elgar, 2006).

Page, E., 'Justice between generations: investigating a sufficientarian approach', *Journal of Global Ethics*, 3 (1) 2007, pp. 3–20.

Parfit, D., 'Equality or priority?', Lindley Lecture, reprinted in M. Clayton and A. Williams (eds), *The Ideal of Equality* (Oxford: Oxford University Press, 2000), pp. 81–125.

Peterson, M. and S. Ove Hansson, 'Equality and priority', *Utilitas*, 17 (3) 2005, pp. 299–309.

Pogge, T., 'Rawls and global justice', *Canadian Journal of Philosophy*, 18 (2) 1988, pp. 227–56.

Pogge, T., *Realizing Rawls* (Ithaca, NY: Cornell University Press, 1989).

Pogge, T., 'Allowing the poor to share the earth', *Journal of Moral Philosophy*, 8 (3) 2011, pp. 335–52.

Rawls, J., 'Outline of a decision procedure for ethics', *Philosophical Review*, 60 (2) 1951, pp. 177–97.

Rawls, J., *The Law of Peoples* (Cambridge, MA: Harvard University Press, 1999).

Rawls, J., *A Theory of Justice*, rev. edn (Cambridge, MA: Harvard University Press, 1999).

Rawls, J., *Justice as Fairness: A Restatement* (Cambridge, MA: Harvard University Press, 2001).

Rawls, J., *Political Liberalism* (New York: Columbia University Press, 2005).

Raz, J., *The Morality of Freedom* (Oxford: Clarendon Press, 1986).

Roemer, J., 'Eclectic distributional ethics', *Politics, Philosophy & Economics*, 3 (3) 2004, pp. 267–81.

Ronzoni, M., 'Two concepts of the basic structure, and their relevance to global justice', *Global Justice: Theory, Practice and Rhetoric*, 1 (2007), pp. 68–85.

Ronzoni, M., 'What makes the basic structure just?', *Res Publica*, 14 (2008), pp. 203–18.

Sangiovanni, A., 'Global justice, reciprocity, and the state', *Philosophy & Public Affairs*, 35 (1) 2007, pp. 3–39.

Satz, D., 'Equality, adequacy, and education for citizenship', *Ethics*, 117 (4) 2007, pp. 623–48.

Scanlon, T. M., 'Rawls on justification', in S. Freeman (ed.), *The Cambridge Companion to Rawls* (Cambridge: Cambridge University Press, 2002), pp. 139–67.

Scanlon, T. M., 'The diversity of objections to inequality', in *The Difficulty of Tolerance: Essays in Political Philosophy* (Cambridge: Cambridge University Press, 2003), pp. 202–18.

Scheffler, S., 'What is egalitarianism?', *Philosophy & Public Affairs*, 31 (1) 2003, pp. 5–39.

Scheffler, S. and V. Munoz-Dardé, 'The division of moral labour', *Proceedings of the Aristotelian Society*, 79 (2005), 229–53, 255–84.

Schemmel, C., 'Distributive and relational equality', *Politics, Philosophy & Economics*, 11 (2) 2012, pp. 123–48.

Schoeman, F., 'Rights of children, rights of parents, and the moral basis of the family', *Ethics*, 91 (1) 1980, pp. 6–19.

Schrag, F., 'Justice and the family', *Inquiry*, 19 (1–4) 1976, pp. 193–208.

Segall, S., 'What is the point of sufficiency?', *Journal of Applied Philosophy*, online first, DOI: 10.1111/japp.12062.

Sen, A., 'Equality of what?', in S. McMurrin (ed.), *The Tanner Lectures on Human Values*, vol. 1 (Salt Lake: University of Utah Press, 1980), pp. 197–220.

Sen, A., 'Poor relatively speaking', *Oxford Economic Papers*, 35 (2) 1983, pp. 153–69.

Sen, A., 'Capability and well-being', in M. Nussbaum and A. Sen (eds), *The Quality of Life* (Oxford: Clarendon Press, 1993), pp. 30–53.

Sen, A., *Development as Freedom* (Oxford: Oxford University Press, 2001).

Sher, G., *Desert* (Princeton, NJ: Princeton University Press, 1989).

Shields, L., *Sufficientarian Bibliography* (2010), <http://liamshields.com/wp-content/uploads/2014/06/Sufficientarian-bibliography.docx> (last accessed 25 March 2016).

Shields, L., 'The prospects for sufficientarianism', *Utilitas*, 24 (1) 2012, pp. 101–17.

Shields, L., 'From Rawlsian autonomy to sufficient opportunity in education', *Politics, Philosophy & Economics*, 14 (1) 2015, pp. 53–66.

207

Shields, L., 'How bad can a good enough parent be?', *Canadian Journal of Philosophy* (forthcoming).

Singer, P., 'Famine, affluence, and morality', *Philosophy & Public Affairs*, 1 (3) 1972, pp. 229–43.

Singer, P., *Practical Ethics* (Cambridge: Cambridge University Press, 1999).

Smith, A., D. Raphael and A. Macfie (eds), *The Theory of the Moral Sentiments* (Oxford: Clarendon Press, 1976).

Steiner, H., 'Territorial justice and global redistribution', in G. Brock and H. Brighouse (eds), *The Political Philosophy of Cosmopolitanism* (Cambridge: Cambridge University Press, 2005), pp. 28–38.

Tan, K.-C., *Justice Without Borders: Cosmopolitanism, Nationalism, and Patriotism* (Cambridge: Cambridge University Press, 2004).

Tan, K.-C., 'Luck, institutions, and global distributive justice: a defence of global luck egalitarianism', *European Journal of Political Theory*, 10 (3) 2011, pp. 394–421.

'Teenage Jehovah's Witness "died after refusing blood"', BBC News, <http://news.bbc.co.uk/1/hi/england/west_midlands/8690785.stm> (last accessed 17 March 2016).

Temkin, L., 'Equality, priority or what?', *Economics and Philosophy*, 19 (1) 2003, pp. 61–87.

Temkin, L., 'Egalitarianism defended', *Ethics*, 113 (4) 2003, pp. 764–82.

'TV star's baby handed to gorillas', BBC News, <http://news.bbc.co.uk/1/hi/england/kent/3258811.stm> (last accessed 17 March 2016).

Unger, P., *Living High and Letting Die: Our Illusion of Innocence* (New York: Oxford University Press, 1996).

Vallentyne, P., 'The rights and duties of childrearing', *William and Mary Bill of Rights Journal*, 11 (3) 2003, pp. 911–1009.

Velleman, D., 'Family history', *Philosophical Papers*, 34 (3) 2005, pp. 357–78.

Walzer, M., *Spheres of Justice: A Defense of Pluralism and Equality* (New York: Basic Books, 1983).

Weirlich, P., 'Utility tempered with equality', *Noûs*, 17 (3) 1983, pp. 423–39.

Widerquist, K., 'How the sufficiency minimum becomes a social maximum', *Utilitas*, 22 (4) 2010, pp. 474–80.

Williams, A., 'Incentives, inequality and publicity', *Philosophy and Public Affairs*, 27 (3) 1998, pp. 225–47.

Williams, A., 'Equality, ambition, and insurance', *Proceedings of the Aristotelian Society*, 78 (1) 2004, pp. 131–50.

Williams, A., 'Liberty, equality, and property', in J. Dryzek, B. Honig and A. Philips (eds), *The Oxford Handbook of Political Theory* (Oxford: Oxford University Press, 2006), pp. 488–506.

Wolff, J., 'Equality: the recent history of an idea', *Journal of Moral Philosophy*, 4 (1) 2007, pp. 125–36.

Woodard, C., 'Enough of enough', unpublished, <https://sites.google.com/site/patternreasons/EnoughofEnough.pdf?attredirects=0> (last accessed 24 March 2016).

Index

Page numbers followed by n refer to notes, and those followed by t are tables